THE TRIUMPH OF WIT

The Triumph of Wit

Molière and Restoration Comedy

Harold C. Knutson

Ohio State University Press
Columbus

Plate I is reproduced from M. Summers, *The Restoration Theatre* (London, 1934), an enhanced version of the original Wren design (held in the Library of All Souls College, Oxford). Plates II, IV, and V are reproduced courtesy of the Collections of the Comédie-Française (Paris). Plate III, from the plates for the article "Théâtre" in *Encyclopédie* by Diderot et al., is reproduced courtesy of the Library of the University of British Columbia.

Engravings 1–4, 6–12, 14, 16–18, and 20–24 are reproduced from the Brissart engravings for *Les Oeuvres de Monsieur de Molière* (Paris, 1682, 8 vols.). Engraving 5 is reproduced by permission of William Andrews Clark Memorial Library, University of California, Los Angeles. Engravings 13, 15, and 19 are reproduced by permission of Houghton Library, Harvard University.

Library of Congress Cataloging-in-Publication Data

Knutson, Harold C.
  The triumph of wit.

  Bibliography: p.
  Includes index.
  1. Molière, 1622–1673—Criticism and interpretation. 2. Molière, 1622–1673—Influence. 3. English drama—Restoration, 1660–1700—History and criticism. 4. English drama (Comedy)—History and criticism. 5. Manners and customs in literature. I. Title.
PQ1860.K53 1987   842'.4   87–1558
ISBN 0-8142-0438-4

This book is dedicated to the memory of
Will G. Moore

CONTENTS

ILLUSTRATIONS

Plates follow page 32

Engravings follow page 147

Unless otherwise indicated, the engravings are those by Brissart for the 1682 edition of Molière's complete works. The dates are the month and year of the first performance.

ix

ACKNOWLEDGMENTS

I have had much help from many sources in the preparation of this book, but I must express special gratitude to the University of British Columbia for the study leaves it awarded me; the Social Sciences and Humanities Research Council of Canada for its generous leave fellowships and research grants; Philippe Sellier for his unfailing moral support; a perceptive and meticulous editorial assistant, Les Koritz; a proficient, dependable typist and word-processor, Penny Hanson; and to Simone, my wife, who believed as always.

INTRODUCTION

For nearly half a century, the subject of Molière and the Restoration theater has lain dormant. The last book of any scope on the matter, John Wilcox's study published in 1938,[1] marks effectively the end of a protracted period of speculation about the English theater's indebtedness to the French dramatist. During this long debate, going back ultimately to the Restoration itself, the obvious borrowings by Restoration playwrights were often magnified into such wholesale plundering that their comedies were seen as little more than rickety pseudo-Gallic structures built of stolen materials, or dismissed as inconsequential touches added to a thoroughly English edifice.[2]

A more moderate position developed as well, eschewing accusations of plagiarism but asserting a more diffuse French influence. Edmund Gosse, in a controversial article on George Etherege,[3] argued that the playwright endeavored to adapt Molière's comedy of manners to the English stage; since Etherege was a major influence upon later Restoration dramatists, it followed that the whole of Restoration comedy carried Molière's imprint. This thesis was taken up more systematically by Dudley Miles in what is no doubt the most important book on the question of indebtedness, *The Influence of Molière on Restoration Comedy*, published in 1910.[4] "Restoration comedy taken as a type," he contends, "owed its inception and found its development in an imitation of the comedy of manners of Molière" (p. 221). It must be said that Miles argues neither massive influence nor rampant pillaging; on the contrary, he is at pains to acknowledge areas—plot development and dialogue, for instance—where Molière's imprint is slight. He even concedes that Restoration comedy could have evolved from elements apparent in earlier English comedy and "that the Restoration would have produced a comedy not much different from the actual product, even had Molière never lived"; but the evidence suggests that the English comedy of manners "owed a good deal to Molière" (p. 220). The modest phrase "a good deal" epitomizes Miles's basically cautious approach to generalizations.

On the other hand, his appended list of borrowings is in the old quantifying school and does suggest, as Wilcox maintains, "that almost all Restoration comedy was deeply indebted to Molière" (p. 12). In his own rebuttal of Miles, Wilcox concludes categorically that the French dramatist "made no significant contribution to the type of comedy we associate with the Restoration" (p. 6). These opposing positions are all the more striking because they arise in part from similar statistical assessments: Miles adduces fifty-seven instances of borrowings from the period 1660–1700, and Wilcox acknowledges that thirty-three Restoration plays contain borrowings from Molière and that five show possible indebtedness. Miles's figure is appreciably higher than Wilcox's, but in the light of the two hundred-or-so comedies that survive from the Restoration, both totals are rather slender.

The question of influence, however, goes beyond mere quantification. When is a borrowing seminal and when it is a mere echo? What is the critical mass at which point an aggregate of borrowed elements becomes a general influence? Obviously, qualitative distinctions must be made in any listing of presumed borrowings. Miles is certainly more than casual in his approach; for him influence seems a matter grasped intuitively and thus needs no explicit conceptual framework. Wilcox, on the other hand, circumscribes his argument with numerous terminological caveats. Some of them are convincing, but others can be readily challenged. Criterion I, for instance, asserts that "the degree of influence depends

upon the extent and centrality of the borrowed elements in the
works of the source" (p. 31; underlined in text). But who is to
determine "centrality" and according to what criteria? Such a
judgment can rest only on a priori, subjective considerations; Wilcox himself banishes from Molière's core inspiration "the farces,
the comedies of intrigue, parts of the comédies ballets, and much
of the cleverness and skill of the great comedies" (p. 32)—
exclusions that to us can appear only as an arbitrary, procrustean
exercise.

Although the influence question cannot be ignored—it is inseparable from a great quantity of scholarship linking Molière to
Restoration comedy—it is readily apparent why it has fallen from
favor. Recent books touch upon the matter only tangentially if at
all. Dobrée had refused to enter the debate as far back as 1924.[5]
Fujimura's influential *The Restoration Comedy of Wit* (1952)[6] alludes
only three times to Molière. Kenneth Muir's little study of the
comedy of manners (1970) notes only that Molière's influence has
been exaggerated.[7] David Hirst repeats a few familiar points of
comparison in the introductory pages to his own book on manners
comedy (1979).[8] Norman Holland does discuss Molière briefly, but
his concluding formulation may be taken as representative: "Although isolated situations, bits of dialogue, and particular characters were borrowed from Molière and other French writers, the
major plays of the period represent an essentially English combination of Ben Jonson's realism with John Fletcher's sophistication."[9]

The influence debate has proved not only inconclusive but it
has diverted attention away from the obvious point that on both
sides of the Channel, at roughly the same period in history, we
were given a legacy of brilliant, enduring monuments to the art
of comedy. In the final analysis, it matters little which is indebted
to which: Wilcox's term *relation* can be taken as not only historical
but conceptual as well: how does Molière *relate* to Restoration
comedy in terms of comic technique, comic vision? For fifty years
this question has not been systematically addressed,[10] and the purpose of the following inquiry is to remedy this neglect.

The truism that culture is inseparable from the social and political climate that nourishes it is all the more evident in the case of theater, not only a cultural product but a social ritual as well. On both sides of the Channel, we find remarkable affinities for the period that concerns us. Both Molière's comedy and that of the Restoration come into being after a period of turmoil—*La Fronde* and the more traumatic Great Rebellion—and in a phase of monarchy dedicated largely to the pleasure principle. An easy, self-indulgent epicureanism held sway, the courtly example eagerly emulated by the Town Wits in London, the Paris gentry in the French capital. Lavish display, untrammeled hedonism went hand in hand with a highly ritualized social life minutely regulated by a complex set of unspoken rules. Kingly etiquette set the tone for Town decorum. What Peter Holland says of Charles II—"[He] combined the rituals of majesty with the freedom of instinctual action"[11]—can be equally applied to the young Louis XIV, heady with the power and authority that fell to him upon Mazarin's death in 1661. Most importantly, both monarchs sponsored theatrical entertainment enthusiastically. Indeed, without Louis XIV's support, moral as well as financial—the king was godfather to Molière's firstborn child—the playwright's Paris career could well have foundered.

Because plays reflect life, we should expect some degree of resemblance between Molière and Restoration comedy. But drama imitates art too, and differing formative influences will perforce engender very different theatrical products, whatever affinity may be shared in social climate. English comedy springs from different roots than its counterpart; moreover, the distinctive training, theatrical identity, and creative personality we find in Molière give his work a quality *sui generis*.

Molière's Paris career dates from 1658, just two years before Charles returned to London from exile. But a good deal of theatrical life already lay behind the thirty-six-year-old Paris-born actor and author. He was barely twenty when he formed the Illustre Théâtre with members of the Béjart family who were to be life-

long associates: Madeleine, a faithful companion and versatile actress, was to share almost his whole career time—she died one year
to the day before Molière himself; a younger Béjart, Armande—
probably Madeleine's sister, possibly her illegitimate daughter—
would become his wife in 1662. The early theatrical venture
proved to be ill-fated and shortly led to voluntary exile from the
capital. From about 1644–45 to 1658, Molière and his company
wandered about the provinces, mainly in the south of France.
These years of growing acting skill and an increased leadership
role, in addition to the first stirrings of creativity—*L'Etourdi* and
Le Dépit amoureux date from this period—culminated in the great
breakthrough: "Monsieur," Louis XIV's younger brother, was so
impressed by a chance meeting with Molière's company that he
offered to sponsor a Paris career. Molière thus returned to his
birthplace in 1658 as director and principal actor of *la troupe de
Monsieur, frère unique du Roi.*

Success in Paris was almost immediate. Molière's skill as a
commedia dell'arte clown—he was later accused of being but a rep-
lica of Scaramouche, the great Italian type actor—shone forth in
the farce *Le Docteur amoureux* with which he won the king's approval at the Louvre in October 1658. The theatergoing public of the
capital was quick to appreciate his talents as well. After a short
stint at the Palais-Bourbon theater, he made the Palais-Royal his
personal bailiwick until his death. As the years went by, he was
called upon, with ever-increasing demands upon his energy, to
entertain both "la Cour et la Ville" in a wide-ranging repertory of
past classics (e.g., Corneille's *Nicomède*, which he performed before the king along with *Le Docteur amoureux*) as well as new plays
like Racine's first two tragedies *La Thébaïde* (1664) and *Alexandre*
(1665), both performed at the Palais-Royal for the first time. At
the same time, his own creations formed a greater and greater part
of his repertory. To name only a few categories and representative
plays: one-act farces like *Les Précieuses ridicules* and *Sganarelle*; well-
wrought five-act plays in verse ("les belles comédies") like *Le
Misanthrope, Tartuffe,* and *Les Femmes savantes*; full-length prose

comedies such as *Dom Juan* and *L'Avare*; *comédies-ballets* in the vein of *Le Bourgeois gentilhomme* and *Le Malade imaginaire*; lively three-act Italianate contributions like *Le Médecin malgré lui* and *Les Fourberies de Scapin*; not to mention a number of occasional pieces contrived for the court like *La Princesse d'Elide* and *Les Amants magnifiques*.

While keeping alive the timeless comic tradition of Italian farce in which he was early nurtured, Molière turned more and more to topical matters by which the spectator could relate comedy to his own world, to life around him. Thus Molière's satire of human folly took increasingly the form of specific, recognizable faults encoded in the social fabric of the time: *préciosité*, social-climbing, dubious religious practices, medical incompetence, avarice as it could be exemplified in the 1660s, and the like. This documentary aspect enlivened by a sure sense of comic caricature—the ingredients of *la comédie de moeurs*, in short—is probably Molière's most distinctive contribution to the art of comedy and parallels, as we shall see, the great manners tradition in Restoration comedy.

On the whole, Molière's career must be reckoned a success, both in terms of his company's reputation and its revenues. La Grange calculated that during his fourteen-year association with Molière, he received, as his share of receipts, just over 50,000 livres, or nearly 3,700 annually[12]—a very substantial income probably approximated by other established actors in the company (by contrast, an urban laborer could earn as little as two livres a month). Molière's own earnings were substantially higher because he often could add an author's share to his own as a player. Not that his Paris life was devoid of ups and downs, however. Much has been written about his presumed domestic tribulations, but there is no direct evidence that he was profoundly unhappy with Armande, notwithstanding a twenty-year age difference. More to the point are his career disappointments: his failure as a tragic actor, the galling public indifference to his serious effort *Dom Garcie de Navarre*, the libellous *ad hominem* attacks occasioned by *L'Ecole des femmes* (including the innuendo that he had married his own bastard daughter), the five-year banning of *Tartuffe*, his failing health. He died ironically at the height of his fame and success, in circumstances too well known to require much elaboration: indisposed toward the end of the fourth performance on 17 February 1673 of *Le Malade imaginaire*, during one of the most triumphant and lucrative runs of his entire career, he was taken to his dwelling on rue Richelieu, to die that evening of internal hemorrhaging. He had just turned fifty-one the month before.

Molière was in his grave, then, before the great Restoration comedies were staged. But his successors kept his plays firmly in the French repertory even after a later generation of comic writers—Regnard and Dancourt—came into the picture. One can well consider Molière as a living presence and an inspiration in France during the whole forty-year period of the Restoration, and far beyond, needless to say.

Only two years after the beginnings of Molière's Paris career, Charles returned to London to assume the crown after the collapse of the Commonwealth. The theaters, closed since 1642, reopened to spectators famished for worldly entertainment after the solemn years of Puritanism. Company managers drew upon all sources in a frantic effort to sate this appetite. English playwrights of preceding ages were pressed into service, even if their work, like Shakespeare's, had to be modified to fit new tastes. Molière was the most important foreign playwright to be exploited both in translation and in anglicized adaptations. A yet more significant homage, visiting companies from France staged Molière in his own language until well into the next century.[13]

Playwrights of the Restoration responded quickly and copiously to this demand; some two hundred comedies alone are extant from the period (a figure that includes, however, translations and adaptations from other sources).[14] That Restoration tastes were wide-ranging is nowhere more apparent than in the variety of this comic production. Just as Molière's enduring masterpieces thrust his fellow writers of comedy into oblivion, so the scintillation of a handful of plays makes us forget the overwhelming majority of extant comedies from the Restoration. These plays exemplify no fewer than seven "schools of comic invention," as Allardyce Nicoll calls them: (1) the comedy of humors, or satire, continuing the Jonsonian tradition; (2) romantic comedy harking back to Elizabethan times; (3) comedy of intrigue in the Spanish style; (4) a hybrid manners-intrigue type sponsored by Dryden; (5) the full-blown comedy of manners; (6) Italianate farce; and (7) sentimental comedy anticipating the major trend of the eighteenth century. We may safely conclude that in terms of quantity and variety, Restoration comedy defies heavy-handed schematization; Nicoll himself cautions us that the seven tendencies are by no means clearly separable (p. 183).

A bewildering variety, then, and elusive of classification. Yet, when we pass from the period piece to the living stage, from the potboiler to the masterpiece, time has done its own sorting out. It is universally acknowledged that the greatest flowering of comedy was in the manners tradition dominated by three playwrights: George Etherege (1636–92), William Wycherley (1641–1716) and William Congreve (1670–1729). None was prolific by comparison with Molière's frenetic output, nor were these English dramatists true men of the theater as was the Frenchman, or Jonson and Shakespeare before them. Their total production—by-products of a life dedicated to other pursuits—amounts to less than half of Molière's, about a dozen comedies in all.

Every scholar has proposed a rather impressionistic list of his own preferences among the "big three" and other dramatists. Ashley Thorndyke, for example, in his sturdy 1929 volume *English Comedy*,[15] list nine "perfect specimens of the comedy of manners":

Etherege	*The Man of Mode*	1676
Wycherley	*The Country Wife*	1675
Congreve	*The Double Dealer*	1693
	Love for Love	1695
	The Way of the World	1699
Vanbrugh	*The Relapse*	1696
	The Provok'd Wife	1697

Farquhar	*The Recruiting Officer*	1706
	The Beaux' Stratagem	1707

(The last two he labels "afterpieces acted beyond the time the period should properly close" [p. 340]).

As is usual in such matters of personal taste, one cannot refrain from cavilling. It is unduly restrictive to limit the master list, as does Norman Holland, to the "first modern comedies" of the three great (p. 7): Vanbrugh certainly deserves his place on Thorndyke's list, but Farquhar's transitional comedies probably less so. Yet at least two exclusions by Thorndyke are hard to explain, that of Etherege's *She Would if She Could* (1668) and of Wycherley's *The Plain Dealer* (1676). The former piece, so warmly praised by Thorndyke himself (p. 25), is acknowledged by almost everyone as the brilliant prototype of Restoration manners comedy. *The Plain Dealer*, though possibly indeed "too serious and satiric" (p. 341), is extolled in every book on manners comedy. Perhaps a conflation of the above preferences will give us a representative yet manageable list of significant manners comedies from which examples can be drawn without either too much repetition or too much dispersal.

So far "comedy of manners" has been used as a loose tag to designate a cluster of plays held to share certain characteristics. When subjected to close scrutiny, the term, like most broad literary categories, eludes easy definition. For one thing, the label itself is an anachronism, invented by Charles Lamb in the Victorian era. As Norman Holland points out, the Restoration knew the subspecies as "genteel comedy," that is, comedy depicting the upper classes (p. 12). As an added problem, almost all the words used to paraphrase manners comedy, like "artificial"—or "realistic," for that matter—are subject to challenge; and the term itself has been criticized as a misnomer: "comedy of wit," according to Thomas Fujimura, comes much closer to the distinctive quality of these plays. I will attempt in chapter 2 to come to grips with this terminological problem. For the moment, it may suffice to point out the salient feature of the genre, one that nobody is likely to contest: a manners comedy has its setting typically in the time and place of the audience. There is no spatial or temporal distance, no exotic locale, no remoteness in history or in a fabled golden age. The playwright is generally at pains to underline the commonality of the world of the play and that of the audience by specific allusions to contemporary reality, to prevailing fashions—*manners*, in short—that the spectator will instantly recognize.

All of the great manners comedies of Restoration England are thus situated in contemporary London (the sole exceptions being the two by Farquhar), and the audience is constantly reminded of customary habits standing out in its own field of observation. There emerges no objective, panoramic view of a teeming metropolis numbering some half-million souls; we are far from the democratic realism of modern literature. The social stratum of English manners comedy is a rarefied, upper-class one depicting "gentlemen" and "gentlewomen" leading a refined, hedonistic existence in the fashionable areas of the Town. Self-indulgent idleness, posturing cynicism, competitive brilliance, and unabashed elitism give manners comedy its distinctive flavor. The common people are kept at a safe distance except as episodic figures like servants, or the orange-woman so contemptuously treated by Dorimant at the beginning of *The Man of Mode*. The mercantile world of the City is hardly mentioned, and a "citizen" draws only disdain when he happens to intrude into genteel circles. In short, an aristocratic coterie takes the social lead and judges all others by its own criteria (this London-centered standard is reflected in *The Beaux' Stratagem* as well). Those who do not belong are excluded, or if they insist on sharing the stage, they become the butt of sneering asides or patronizing irony. We repeatedly come across fops, fools, country bumpkins, superannuated coquettes, and the like; they draw both the derisive laughter of the people of breeding on stage and hoots from an audience fully aware of the code by which its world is being interpreted.

It is this type of comedy that Miles saw as an "imitation" of Molière (p. 221). More recent scholars correctly point out that earlier English comedy itself contains the seeds of the manners tradition.[16] But whatever the origin of the Restoration comedy of manners, no one can deny its affinity with Molière, the first great dramatist in France to integrate the depiction of manners into the fabric of existing forms of comedy. Corneille's comedies anticipate, it is true, many features of the manners genre and were a significant influence on Molière himself, but they remain period pieces of essentially historical interest, in contrast to Molière's enduring masterpieces.[17]

Without losing sight of the fact that Molière moved Proteus-like from one dramatic form to another in his career, we are entitled then to investigate the manners aspect of his theater. Once again we beg the question to be discussed in chapter 2—What is manners comedy?—but for the moment we may return to the basic criterion of the genre and apply it to Molière: which of his works present to the audience its own time and space? As it turns out, about half of Molière's comedies are set in Paris (or in nearby Versailles) and in the time frame of the spectator:

Les Précieuses ridicules	1659
Sganarelle	1660
L'Ecole des maris	1661
Les Fâcheux	1661
L'Ecole des femmes	1662

(Locale is not specifically mentioned, but a setting in the capital is plausible: a 1734 printing does indicate "la scène est à Paris.")

La Critique de l'Ecole des femmes	1663

(Again, ostensibly a Paris drawing room.)

L'Impromptu de Versailles	1663
L'Amour médecin	1665
Le Misanthrope	1666
Tartuffe	1667–69
L'Avare	1668
Monsieur de Pourceaugnac	1669

Le Bourgeois gentilhomme	1670
Les Femmes savantes	1671
Le Malade imaginaire	1673

A substantial number of Molière's plays representing his major subgenres and including most of his masterpieces encompass, then, a basic feature of manners comedy. The potential for a valid, productive comparison with English comedy appears evident. Yet criticism, especially on the Anglo-Saxon side, has been dominated by a tenacious conventional wisdom: other than a vague concern with the contemporary life-style of the social and political center, English manners comedy and Molière's *comédies de moeurs* share little. An older generation of commentators, for instance, had affirmed a moral and aesthetic superiority in the Frenchman in order to underline more reprovingly the license and slapdash dramaturgy of the manners school. This stance echoed the Victorian prudishness that virtually banished Restoration comedy from the stage for many decades. Vestiges of nineteenth-century moralism remain even in modern comparisons with Molière. Thus Allardyce Nicoll, in his imposing *History of Restoration Drama*, published in 1923, lauds Molière's "free and easy laughter," so different from the forced hilarity of the Restoration (p. 178); a "fine humanitarian spirit" totally at odds with the immorality and snobbishness of Restoration heroes and heroines dominates Molière's theater; the confused, multilinear, busy plots of English plays cannot compare to Molière's "delicate three-act cameo, unified and harmonious" (ibid.). But it would be unfair to portray such an eminent scholar as a mere throwback to Macaulay, one of the most vocal Victorian adversaries of Restoration comedy; for all of his admiration for Molière (based, it must be said, on a very narrow sampling of the playwright's work) and his distaste of Restoration excess, he describes accurately and impartially the basic features of manners comedy.

This overall broadmindedness has become, fortunately, characteristic of all recent scholarship on Restoration comedy. Indignation over its alleged obscenity has faded away in today's tolerant world; at worst, Restoration comedy is merely "trivial, gross and dull," as L. C. Knights affirmed iconoclastically not too long ago.[18] In consequence, Molière is no longer seen as a supremely decorous model worthy of emulation. There is greater awareness as well of the breadth and variety of comic expression in his own theater; alongside the polish of *Le Misanthrope*, for instance, and the humanitarian thrust of his comedies in general, one cannot help draw attention to the priapic Sganarelle of *Le Médecin malgré lui* or the less-than-humane treatment Molière metes out to such hapless figures as Monsieur de Pourceaugnac or George Dandin.

The more important reason adduced to explain the basic incompatibility of Molière and Restoration manners comedy relates to *Weltanschauung*, the social and philosophical underpinnings of his plays. Whereas Restoration comedy was acknowledged to depict specific mores from an upper-class viewpoint, English scholarship tended to depict Molière as a satirist stigmatizing vice and folly in general in accordance with timeless common sense. Thus Miles in 1910 presented a down-to-earth Molière embodying the norms of the mercantile world into which he was born (pp. 20–21). Kathleen Lynch's seminal work *The Social Mode of Restoration Comedy* (1927) placed Molière in strong antithesis to the aristocratic social orientation of Restoration comedy; the Frenchman "is mainly interested in the opposition of affected, insincere people who are positive fools, and candid, sensible people who have attained maturity of wisdom like his own" (p. 9). For John Wilcox, English manners comedy depicts "the sensual, witty, fashionable, disillusioned courtiers" whereas Molière projects the ethos of "the middle-class Parisian" (p. 194).

Such generalizations about Molière's theater become rarer as we advance into recent scholarship. Since interest in influence has virtually disappeared, questions of overall similarity or remoteness lose their value as a tool of comparison or contrast. Indeed, save for the inevitable comments relating *L'Ecole des femmes* to *The Country Wife* and *Le Misanthrope* to *The Plain Dealer*, little is said about Molière at all in the most recent books on Restoration comedy or the manners tradition. For that very reason, earlier generalizations have not been contested or revised, notwithstanding the great leap forward in Molière scholarship during the 1940s and 1950s. For generations French scholarship, in parallel with the trends just noted in Anglo-Saxon criticism, had steadfastly portrayed the dramatist as a moralist-philospher. The generality of his satire, coupled with the apparent didacticism of his *raisonneurs*, was adduced as supporting evidence, along with what was perceived as mundane, commonsense wisdom, a quality that identified him with middle-class seriousness. This latter-day nineteenth-century dogma effectively collapsed in the aftermath of two postwar seminal studies. In 1949 Will G. Moore laid to rest the antiquated image of the worthy sage, the philosophizing dramatist, and in its place offered us the comic artist, the man whose main objective was to write entertaining, stageworthy comedies.[19] René Bray enlarged upon this perspective in his significantly titled *Molière homme de théâtre* (1954).[20]

Still another landmark work, more germane to our purposes, dates from the same period (1948): Paul Bénichou's *Morales du grand siècle*, with its illuminating chapter on Molière.[21] Bénichou's now familiar thesis holds that Molière actually reflects an aristocratic *Weltanschauung*, an elitist spirit in strong contrast to any concept of middle-class common sense or average wisdom. The bourgeois in his theater, far from being models for emulation, are unfailingly ridiculed as mean-spirited, narrow-minded, domineering—the very antithesis of an upper-class ideal of magnanimity, liberality, and social distinction. Bénichou's contention, revolutionary though it may have seemed, is founded on historical plausibility: how indeed could a dramatist who conceived so many plays on royal command present to a king like Louis XIV anything but a laudatory, glorified image of the social hierarchy? How, in a society dominated by a small, exclusive elite—"La Cour et la Ville"—could Molière do otherwise than cater to the well-bred and the powerful and reflect back to them either their own idealized image or a caricature of any transgression of their code? The ramifications of this change of perspective have been momentous. Scholars have increasingly focused their attention upon the seventeenth-century aristocratic norms as they are given concrete expression in Molière's theater. Concern for social decorum, for worldly propriety, has come to the fore to compete with other recent approaches in Molière criticism.[22] A major consequence has been the interest in Molière's codification of *honnêteté,* the great classical ideal of civility arguably more concerned with the imperatives of social interaction than with rules of abstract morality.[23] Thus the excesses stigmatized by Molière may be related not only to philosophical ideas or moral notions but also to breaches of behavior, betrayals of precise norms enshrined in social practice of the time.

The recent development of a sociocritical approach to Molière has consolidated this interest in social background.[24] This methodology has drawn upon trailblazing studies in social history by such eminent French scholars as Roland Mousnier, Robert Mandrou, and Pierre Goubert. As a result of their painstaking research, a clearer, more accurate picture of social strata has emerged, together with a more systematic assessment of outward manifestations of hierarchy and privilege. It is now abundantly evident, for example, that the French middle class of Molière's time, far from claiming distinction on its own terms and promoting its own "philosophy," was inclined to spend vast sums to buy upper-class status and prerogatives.

More importantly, sociocriticism provides a way of removing the stigma of triviality and artificiality that still lingers around the concept of "manners"; at the same time, it deepens the often shallow interpretations of *comédie de moeurs,* a term oscillating frequently between a rather anachronistic emphasis on realism and an imprecise notion of social satire. In the view of the sociocritic, cultural indices embedded in drama provide for the spectator a stimulating and basic process of comparison. "The greater the number and significance of the indicators, the greater the opportunity to evaluate a character's actions and ideas to others of his station" (Gaines, p. 83). The comedy of manners depends on this process for its appeal, and it is significant that the principle so long recognized in English manners comedy—the portrayal of contrasting patterns of social behavior as embodied in various characteristic social types—should be now so convincingly applied to Molière's theater.

To be sure, the objective analysis of behavioral standards and the comic representation of reality are two different things; the natural tendency of the comic vision is to distort reality in the direction both of idealization and caricature. True, comic theory in the seventeenth century stressed the mimetic role of the genre; pictorial imagery abounds in the playwrights' own conceptions: "la peinture de la conversation des honnêtes gens" (Corneille); "il faut peindre d'après nature" (Molière). But in actual practice, the business of a comic playwright is not primarily to document reality but to promote laughter; the comic world we see before us may bear only an oblique resemblance to social fact. E. E. Stoll's admonition of long ago is still pertinent: "Literature reflects the taste of the time rather than the time itself, and often the two are widely different. We like what we are not, or we are not what we think we are. Literature is, of course, not life, neither history or material for history, but . . . a life within life. . . ."[25]

To conclude this prolegomenon:

If then Molière conceived much of his theater in the matrix of upper-class values; if an important feature of these plays is the comic depiction of social practice—*manners*, in a profound and renewed sense—then we could have a species of comedy in fundamental harmony with the "coterie" manners comedy that took shape in England during Molière's lifetime. There are differences in comic technique, to be sure; no one can claim that Molière and the playwrights of the Restoration wrote identical versions of manners comedy. But in terms of world view, of social relevance, a deep kinship may be postulated between two comic productions hitherto held to have little common measure. The validation of that assumption will be the business of the following chapters.

As within all of Restoration theater we have delimited a particular subspecies conventionally labeled manners comedy, so with Molière we must circumscribe a vein of comparable *comédie de moeurs* within an extremely varied comic production encompassing much that escapes the manners category. Molière's Greek *divertissements—La Princesse d'Elide* and *Les Amants magnifiques*, for instance—may convey an idealized image of the French court and therefore refer indirectly to contemporary mores; but we are in a distant, never-never land presenting few signs that carry specific social meaning and consequently few of the contrasts in social practice that characterize manners comedy. The Molière plays to be discussed in this study will be first of all those taking place in Paris. As befits plays set in the capital and in the spectator's time, all allude explicitly to recognizable mores; even the farcical *Sganarelle* distinguishes between fashionable literature like *Clélie* and boringly didactic tracts ("moralités"), examples of which are specifically mentioned (vv. 28–40). Norms of behavior and breaches of them are represented by a complex of indices both textual and visual. As for the latter, contemporary iconographical evidence regarding costume and décor will be frequently adduced. The engravings produced by Brissart for the 1682 edition of Molière's complete works provide an invaluable source of visual indicators. In addition, we have frontispieces for a total of six comedies published at various times during the dramatist's lifetime. There remains as well other scattered evidence, both visual and verbal, that will be brought to the fore as the argument unfolds.

In this respect it must be noted that density of social indicators does not alone signify the manners tradition in comedy. As a drama about noble *dérogeance*, *Dom Juan* teems, as Gaines demonstrates, with precise allusions to noble exemplarity (pp. 95–111). Yet the play is obviously not a comedy of manners; apart from questions of tone and denouement, the signs have to be interpreted through an indeterminate spatial and temporal setting. Thus, to a degree *Dom Juan* resembles such Italianate plays as *Les Fourberies de Scapin*. On the other hand, other plays set outside the capital may present such a strong Paris reference point that by implication they are Paris comedies. *George Dandin* and *La Comtesse d'Escarbagnas* are prime examples. And even a country farce like *Le Médecin malgré lui* encodes Paris manners in its costuming: young Léandre is shown in a contemporary engraving dressed as a typical gallant of the capital. To balance, then, the dozen or so Restoration masterpieces mentioned earlier (pp. 8–9), I shall be concerned with those fifteen or twenty Molière plays that, like the English ones, are built on a structure of social indicators that the spectator interprets through a commonly held vision of proper behavior and, just as importantly, through a collective comic process of distortion, schematization, and antithesis. The approach to be applied in the following pages is already a commonplace of English scholarship, whereas its appropriateness for the Frenchman, not yet systematically demonstrated, will be the chief contention of this study. The manners masterpieces from England will play an important, but secondary, role as illustrations of conceptual criteria and as evidence of a shared *Weltanschauung*.

Drama, however, cannot be analyzed in the abstract. Not only must the playwright accede to the wishes and expectations of the audience, without whose financial support his career would be short-lived, but he must likewise accept the material apparatus that gives concrete, immediate shape to his vision. Without an actor, a playing space, and spectator, drama is only literature. A proper study of Molière and his kinship with the Restoration theater would not be meaningful without some attention to the contemporary comic stage in Paris and London.

Chapter 1

THE COMIC STAGE
IN PARIS AND LONDON

To a large degree, a composite picture of the stage used by Molière and that on which Restoration comedies were performed can be obtained only by inference and conjecture. Most of what we know comes from a potpourri of information conveyed by chance contemporary observations, extant plans and drawings, the internal evidence of the plays themselves, engravings accompanying published dramas, company business records, and the like. What follows, therefore, does not pretend to be an exhaustive or minutely detailed treatment of the question. But enough data are available to suggest, as we shall presently see, a striking resemblance between conditions of staging in the two capitals.

The Restoration playhouse evolved from the enclosed private stage of late Elizabethan and Caroline times.[1] Performers had abandoned the traditional Elizabethan theater open to the sky; the advantage of natural light was little compensation for capricious London weather. The hall, naturally, had to be lit artificially, usually by large numbers of candles. In Paris plays had been staged for more than a century in a comparable enclosed rectangular playhouse known as l'Hôtel de Bourgogne. In Molière's time it housed the most prestigious company in the capital, les comédiens du roi, players who cultivated tragedy in particular and enjoyed pride of preference by both Corneille and Racine. Similar halls sprang up in Paris in the course of the seventeenth century, often remodeled indoor tennis courts or *jeux de paume*. The Théâtre du Marais, for example, had the special distinction of staging Corneille's early dramas including *Le Cid*; but by the 1660s it was eking out a precarious existence presenting spectacular "machine" plays. In 1641 Richelieu inaugurated a sumptuous theater hall in his Palais-Cardinal, the first one in Paris conceived from its inception as a playing space. After a brief stay at the Palais-Bourbon, demolished in 1660 to make room for an enlarged Louvre, Molière made this hall, known later as the Palais-Royal (see plate I), his personal fief, and it remained so until his death, when it became Lully's preserve for opera.

This brief sketch would be incomplete without mention of Les Italiens, the *commedia dell'arte* company which, though not enjoying its own permanent locale, was a major force in Paris theater life. After many visits to the capital by various Italian companies, one troupe settled there in the 1640s and subsequently shared Molière's Palais-Royal. They presented a varied repertory, including, later in the century, topical satire in French; but having incurred the wrath of Louis XIV for alluding to Madame de Maintenon in *La Fausse Prude*, they were banished in 1697. They returned under the regency, however, to renew their hold on the Paris audience.

During Molière's Paris career, then, three theater halls and four companies dominated the stage life of the capital: the Hôtel de Bourgogne, the Marais, and the Palais-Royal, with the latter housing both Molière and the Italiens. When Molière died in 1673, his actors were amalgamated with those of the Marais, and the newly merged company settled in a Left Bank playhouse, l'Hôtel Guénégaud, rue Mazarine. In 1680 the king combined the Hôtel de Bourgogne with the Guénégaud troupe to form the Comédie-Française, the Guénégaud theater being its bailiwick. The new company, when forced to leave its hall in 1687, acquired two years later a magnificent playhouse designed by François d'Orbay and located on what is today la rue de l'Ancienne Comédie (see plates II, III, and IV). In the meantime, the *comédiens italiens* moved into the vacated Hôtel de Bourgogne.

In contrast to Paris, where fierce competition among theater

companies was the rule until 1680, two London entrepreneurs acquired a monopoly over the public stage at the beginning of the
Restoration. Thomas Killigrew formed the King's Company, and
William Davenant directed the fortunes of a group of players
sponsored by the king's brother, the duke of York—the Duke's
Servants. Both men were playwrights with long theatrical experience going back to Caroline times, and both remained loyal to
the monarchy during the events of the interregnum. Killigrew
spent the period of upheaval largely in exile, while Davenant eked
out an existence in England with periodic harassment by the re-
gime in power.

After a start in temporary quarters, Killigrew built a playhouse in Bridges Street, the first Theatre-Royal of 1663. A near-
decade of success and popularity was cut short when a fire de-
stroyed this structure in 1672, a disaster from which the King's
Company never recovered. Killigrew moved into the Lincoln's
Inn Fields playhouse—just vacated by his rival Davenant—before
reopening in a new playhouse, the second Theatre-Royal of 1674
(the one for which, presumably, Wren drew the sectional design
reproduced as plate V). Here he staged with success Wycherley's
Country Wife in 1675 and the same playwright's *Plain-Dealer* a year
later. But poor management, dissension, and other misadventures
drove the fortunes of the company to ever-lower points, and finally the King's Company was saved from an ignominious collapse
by merger with its competitor in 1682. The combined company
used the Theatre-Royal as its venue.

Davenant had indeed fared better with his Duke's Servants.
Until 1672 he had occupied a modified tennis court, the Lincoln's
Inn Fields theater (the first English public playhouse to use scenery). Then his sumptuous Dorset Garden playhouse, designed by
Wren, opened with a reprise of Dryden's popular comedy *Sir Martin Mar-all*, an adaptation of Molière's *L'Etourdi* first staged by the
Duke's Servants in 1667. With his gifted actor Betterton, he scored
a great triumph with Etherege's *Man of Mode* in 1675 and continued
to dominate the London stage until the 1682 Union, two years,

incidentally, after Louis XIV's enforced merger of existing Paris companies into the Comédie-Française. After a period of growing dissension, a group of actors led by Betterton seceded in 1695 to form once again a rival company, based in the old playhouse in Lincoln's Inn Fields. Here Congreve's masterpieces *Love for Love* (1695) and *The Way of the World* (1699) were first staged. Only in 1708 were the competing companies once again united.[2]

Since no two playhouses were exactly alike, it is somewhat hazardous to present a standardized image of the "typical" theater in both cities. On the other hand, it would appear irrelevant to catalogue the often minute variations for the purpose of historical accuracy when a general picture, adequate for our purposes, emerges from available data, especially the iconographic evidence reproduced in the plates. As in all similar theater halls, a basic separation existed between the audience's domain and the players' space, or the stage. The proscenium arch, as well as the curtain, was the conventional mode of signifying this separation. However, the proscenium arch, though characteristic of the Restoration playhouse, was by no means generalized in France; only the Palais-Royal had one (see plate I). The curtain, moreover, though existing in both capitals, was used only for discovering the stage before the performance and hiding it afterward (in London it apparently rose before the prologue and fell after the epilogue).[3] Thus the stage remained open to the audience for the duration of the play, and all scene changes, those between as well as within acts, had to be carried out in full view.

Summers (*Theatre*, p. 94) and Peter Holland (pp. 29–31) emphasize the importance in the Restoration playhouse of the "apron," a forestage that projected into the audience space a considerable distance beyond the proscenium arch. The sectional design by Wren (plate V), adduced by both Summers and Holland as evidence, shows clearly a long, curved apron some seventeen feet deep. On the basis of this material circumstance, Holland generalizes perceptively about the resulting relationship between player and audience. As acting took place almost invariably well down-stage, the player occupied a peculiarly ambiguous space. He was separated from the spectators by the curved edge of the forestage; the audience saw him, moreover, as part of the represented action because he was framed by the proscenium arch behind him and included in the visual field of the décor. Yet the apron, besides giving the impression of being thrust into the audience, was incorporated into the decorative design of the hall; in the Wren drawing, the archway motifs of the side continue right up to the forestage and beyond, stopping only at the proscenium arch, thereby creating a clear visual association between audience space and the forestage.

Consequently, we must speak of three zones in the Restoration theater: the audience space proper, the forestage, and the scenery. The Wren document shows very clearly these linear divisions; the scenic stage was as deep as the forestage in front of it. A similar arrangement seems to be typical in Paris as well. That the playing space is well downstage is clear from iconographic evidence (see plate I as well as the Brissart engravings). A drawing dating from the 1680s and representing a longitudinal section of the theater designed by François d'Orbay (see plate II) shows striking affinities with the Wren plan. It would seem that the forestage shared the decorative pattern of the hall, and that its front line extended at least a few feet beyond the proscenium. Evidence from the mid-eighteenth century indicates that the same theater was remodeled and that the forestage was thrust even farther into the audience's space (fifteen feet or so, or much the same as for the Wren theater), with the orchestra being reduced accordingly (plate III).[4] In the engraving depicting the Palais-Royal (plate I), we find no protruding apron, but a very deep proscenium arch is pictured, perhaps several feet in depth, and also an extension at center stage with steps leading to the pit level. The actors represented appear to be in this downstage area. That the playing space was situated in front of the scenery is further confirmed by an engraving from

1669 representing a scene from *Tartuffe* (Appendix, no. 19*): we clearly see the downstage edge of the angle wing behind the actors on our left.

Another feature of the acting space needs special emphasis. On both sides of the Channel, it was customary to seat spectators *on* the stage. In London the practice had been abandoned at the beginning of the Restoration but returned in about 1690.[5] In Paris this part of the audience, most often members of the gentry, would occupy chairs or benches on either side of the stage. The floor plan for the d'Orbay Theatre (plate IV) shows eight benches on the stage, four on either side of the playing space. If we extrapolate from the scale shown (one *toise* equaled about six feet) and if we allow for crowding, we can imagine the more than one hundred spectators who on many occasions occupied this area. In Molière's time at the Palais-Royal, as many as thirty-six spectators were thus exposed, although eight or ten was more the rule.[6] Since the average stage seems to have been about thirty feet wide, it can be readily imagined that the actual playing space was relatively confined.

As for scenic design, the system used on the Restoration stage made possible the frequent change of locale that is typical of English comedy. To simplify somewhat: the various places to be represented were painted on a series of flats, which were then placed one behind the other at intervals of a few feet (the Wren drawing clearly shows these vertical lines behind the proscenium arch). Split down the middle, the flat could be pulled away on both sides to reveal a new scene. With increasing frequency during the Restoration, the last flat would "discover" a group of characters already in place in the new setting, who would move downstage to continue the play.

*For the purposes of this study, plates relating to the playhouse are referred to by roman numerals and appear at the end of chapter 1 (pp. 33–37); engravings illustrating specific stage settings or costumes are indicated by arabic numbers and appear in the Appendix, since they are referred to throughout the text.

It is often and erroneously thought that Molière's decor was by contrast fixed and abstract, an example of classical respect for unity of place. Roger Herzel, by a careful scrutiny of iconographical evidence, shows convincingly that Molière used no fewer than three different kinds of scenic design.[7] The dominant pattern is shown in the diagram below. Actors could enter and exit upstage or downstage of either angle wing. This pattern fit both the outdoor setting of, say, *L'Ecole des femmes* (Appendix, no. 8), and the private room of a play like *Tartuffe* (Appendix, nos. 19, 20). In the first case, the angle wing represented a house with practical doors and windows, with the backdrop showing a town or garden perspective. In the interior setting, the angle wings, together with the backdrop, depicted the three walls of the room, with the wings angled toward the center to enhance an effect of perspective. Thus Molière's innovative use of the private salon setting in addition to the "maisons et rues" décor did not require a wholesale reconceptualization of scenic practice.

Backdrop

Angle   Angle

Wing   Wing

Playing Space

(Spectators)   (Spectators)

Audience

(Pit)

The second type of stage design involved movable scenery. Molière used such decor changes in his spectacle plays (like *Le*

Malade imaginaire) for the *intermèdes*. But even in straightforward comedies like *Le Sicilien* and *Le Médecin malgré lui* place is by no means strictly unified. The former shows an outdoor, nocturnal setting, but the painting scene (Appendix, no. 16) takes place in a private room; *Le Médecin malgré lui* is set partly out-of-doors in a clearing, partly in front of Géronte's house. Scene changes here were effected by *fermes*, or split flats like those of the Restoration theater, which were pulled aside to reveal a new scene. The play whose design most clearly approximated that of the Restoration is *Dom Juan*, intended to compete with the Italiens. Since the system of multiple *fermes* was characteristic of *commedia dell'arte* stage design, Molière commissioned an elaborate series of huge flats that depicted various scenes in perspective, the closest ones as high as eighteen feet.[8] The d'Orbay floor plan (plate IV) indicates similar equipment to provide for a variety of scenes and for quick changes. In a scenic space of about fifteen feet in depth, there was provision for six wing flats on each side, four backdrops, a fifth backdrop open at the center, and a small *toile de fond* at the very back.

Finally, Herzel stipulates a box set for *Les Précieuses ridicules* and *La Critique de l'Ecole des femmes*, both staged as afterpieces. A separate little setting was used behind a *ferme* that functioned as a backdrop for the main play. When this was pulled aside, a new décor was disclosed, much like the Restoration "discovery" technique.[9] The actors, once having established the locale of the action, would then move downstage for the whole of the short play.

It is important to underline the emblematic nature of scenery in both Paris and London. It was not meant to encompass and define the character, to show a real setting that would confirm the presence of a genuine human being on stage, to encourage, in short, the suspension of disbelief. The action occurred in front of scenery that primarily served a marking, symbolic function. Indeed, the whole relationship between spectator and actor in the practice of seventeenth-century theater points vigorously away from the doctrinaire illusionism that was codified in the abstract

by such theorists as d'Aubignac.[10] Artifice was unabashedly evident on all sides. Scenery no doubt depicted a forced perspective
whose distortion must have been all too obvious. The representation of a garden ostensibly at a great distance could well have been
only twenty feet away. The candelabra distributed above audience
and stage alike ensured a common lighting for the entire playhouse. The practice of plunging spectators into dark, formless anonymity before a brilliantly lit stage could not have been imagined.
The fact that the actor played his role so close to the pit—indeed,
in a space vaguely intrusive from an audience perspective—must
have further underlined the perception of comedy as play, not realistic representation. Again, the effect of beholding spectators on
the stage, often within a few feet of the actors, could not but have
heightened the strong visual association of players and those
played to. Finally, the fact that the audience, in both Paris and
London, was a noisy, unruly crowd of people crammed into a
small, unventilated space—not at all the reverently subdued spectators of today—militated still further against total absorption
into the spectacle.[11]

Thus the actor and his persona existed—especially in comedy—
in a kind of floating relationship, tacitly acknowledged on both
sides. The prologues and epilogues were spoken by the player in
the dress of his role; and when Molière made his post-performance
appearance as an *orateur* to publicize his next attraction, he no
doubt still wore the costume of his character. Yet the actor rarely
stepped outside his role during the play, or explicitly recognized
the presence of the spectator, so that a certain representational
purity was maintained. True, in one memorable instance Molière
made one of his characters blur these distinctions: Harpagon, during
his hysterical tirade at the end of act four, involves the audience in
his quest for his thief: "N'est-il pas caché-là parmi vous? Ils me
regardent tous, et se mettent à rire" (4.7). But this open ambivalence is highly untypical. On the other hand, the presence of the
spectator is the object of continual tacit reference. Without leav-
ing his role, the actor could communicate directly with the au-

dience by such formal devices as the innumerable monologues and asides that characterize Restoration manners comedy. Molière is less consistent in his use of these inexhaustible sources of mirth: *Les Femmes savantes* has none of either. But the aside and its longer version as a soliloquy account for much of the comic impact of *L'Ecole des femmes*, *George Dandin*, and *L'Avare*, for instance. More importantly, even when these specific devices are absent, it is not difficult to imagine lines spoken to another character as being directed, by means of a subtle gesture, a flick of the eyelid, at the spectator as well. In short, we must visualize, on both sides of the Channel, an acting style that played broadly to the audience while safeguarding a nominal and largely superficial illusionism.

Now to the audience itself. The general division of its own space was remarkably parallel in Paris and London, although significant differences of distribution will be noted. In both cases the hall reflected the hierarchical organization of the society that frequented it. The most expensive seats were the most visible ones, those on the stage; here the male gentry sat in showy splendor. Upper-class space was prolonged in Paris into the lower side galleries, from which one could see and be seen; the higher galleries catered to the less noteworthy. An amphitheater opposite the stage was yet one notch below on the social scale. Finally, the pit provided standing room to a motley crowd of lower-class men, although nobles and women were occasionally to be seen there.

In London we find the same hierarchization of audience space, but the actual zones are rather different. Apart from those on the stage, the most prestigious seats were in the boxes that ringed the pit. Just below these in social standing was a combined area grouping seats in the first gallery and the pit. One can explain the higher social standing of the London pit very simply: spectators had benches to sit on. The expedient of providing seats for the Paris *parterre* had to wait until much later. A second gallery provided space at a less prestigious level. Finally, the third gallery catered to the same plebeian elements that in Paris crowded into the pit.

The actual ticket prices were remarkably constant during the period that concerns us. For London the following figures are typical.

Boxes:	four shillings
Pit/first gallery:	two shillings six pence
Second gallery:	one shilling six pence
Third gallery:	one shilling
	(P. Holland, p. 16)

The typical London theater could hold up to a thousand spectators, but full houses were extremely rare. An average audience would have numbered about half that (ibid.). As for the distribution, the following sample figures from an actual 1677 performance of Dryden's *All for Love* (cited in ibid., p. 17) appear to be indicative: boxes, 36; pit and first gallery, 117; second gallery, 63; third gallery, 33. This total attendance of 249 produced box office receipts of 28 pounds, four shillings. (Since English spectators did not sit on the stage at this time, they are naturally not itemized).

Audience size and capacity were rather similar on both sides of the Channel. An entry from Hubert's *registre* may be offered as a comparison, tenuous though it be. This precious record of Molière's 1672–73 season, his last, reflects the fluctuation of audience appeal from play to play, and is therefore difficult to sample in any convincing way. Since the average of ticket sales for individual performances was about four hundred,[12] we might choose with a minimum of arbitrariness the performance on 15 May 1672 (five years before the Dryden performance mentioned above) of *Les Femmes savantes*, for which a total of 428 tickets were sold. The breakdown is as follows:

Théâtre [stage]:	8 at 5 livres 10 sous	44 livres
Loges:	22 at 5 livres 10 sous	121 livres[13]
Amphithéâtre:	14 at 3 livres	42 livres

Loges hautes:	80 at 1 livre 10 sous	121 livres, 10 sous
Loges du 3ème rang:	15 at 1 livre	15 livres
Parterre	289 at 15 sous	216 livres, 15 sous
Total	428 tickets sold	560 livres, 5 sous

The overall breakdown is quite close to the yearlong average attendance in each category. For example, 7% of the spectators were in the *théâtre/loges* sections, as opposed to an average of 8.2%, and 67% were in the *parterre*, compared with the average of 59%. The ratio of the actual house to capacity is quite comparable to that noted for the Restoration theater. A full house in the Palais-Royal was on the order of 1,000, although absolute capacity has been estimated as high as 1,400. Thus the theater was about half full in the above sample. The largest audience for the season was 925 (*Psyché*, 20 November 1672).[14]

The actual social composition of the audience is a matter of ongoing discussion. To a large degree, a persistent fallacy has clouded our perception of the question. It has been assumed that because comedy reflects a particular social stratum and celebrates its values, only members of that segment of society would constitute the audience, and that a change of tone in comedy would therefore indicate a renewed clientele. Thus, Nicoll asserted that the audience of Restoration comedy was largely composed of the flighty and cynical courtiers so vividly depicted in it (p. 8). Similarly, the increased polish and decorum of French comedy in the 1630s, for instance, was accounted for by a conjectured change in audience composition—more women, more upper-class people in general. But careful, impartial research has yielded more reliable data for both Paris and London; and once again, remarkable parallels are to be found. John Lough has demonstrated that the Paris theater audience was quite heterogeneous and reflected in fact a broad spectrum of society from the lackey and soldier to members of great families, including the king (pp. 55–122). Peter Holland has reached similar conclusions for the London audience, which included a far more representative sampling of the population than earlier scholars had supposed (pp. 4–5). One has only to note Pepys's lament about the number of "mean people" who insist on flocking to the playhouse. As Holland suggests, the question is not who attended the plays but who controlled the way comedy presented society (p. 15): however large the citizen audience, the upper-class element saw to it that their values and style of life dominated the genre. Lough presents the same picture for Paris:

> The more aristocratic sections of society . . . were certainly strongly represented in the theatre audiences of the time, and it is their outlook rather than that of the middle layers of society which is more clearly reflected in the drama of the age. . . . To be successful, a play must appeal to . . . *les honnêtes gens.* . . . Thus the drama of the age was strongly influenced by the aristocratic outlook of the society in which it was produced. (p. 161)

The potential audience was, theoretically at least, the entire population, something on the order of half a million in both cities. But the actual number of spectators, even if socially diverse, was very small. The rapid tapering off of box office receipts from given plays in both cities bears witness to an audience potential quickly exhausted; in fact, Holland contends that some spectators, like Pepys, went several times to a play during its run, and that therefore the actual audience was even smaller than the number of tickets sold (p. 7). Lough has conjectured, on the basis of available data, that the Paris theatergoing public could have been as small as 35,000 (p. 51). He disputes with reason the exaggerated inferences made by Lancaster on the sole basis of ticket sales, which could be as high as 150,000 in a year.[15] The Hubert *registre* tells us that for the entire 1672–73 season a total of about 53,000 tickets were sold. This was but one of four companies, of course; but if one takes into account the kind of repeated attendance noted with Pepys, Lough's figure could well be not far off. In any event, since there were two theaters competing for public favor in London during the greatest part of the Restoration, and as many as four companies in Paris during the same period, it can be readily assumed that competition for this limited audience was fierce; the acrimony of the destructive quarrels that pitted Molière against his rivals, for instance, had a foundation in hard economic facts.

It has been my purpose in the foregoing to present only a rapid overview of a complicated picture. This account of the physical theater does suggest, however, that there is a remarkable similarity in both Paris and London as regards the form of the theater, the composition of the audience, and the basic acting conventions for comedy, especially those governing the relationship of audience to spectacle. Although comedy appealed to a variety of social groups on both sides of the Channel, the hierarchical distribution of the spectators inside the theater and the scales of ticket prices that prevailed point to a predominantly elite controlling group imposing (with little resistance, it seems) its own world view on others. It will be the task of the following chapters to validate these assumptions in the texts of the plays themselves.

Plate I. Palais–Royal playhouse

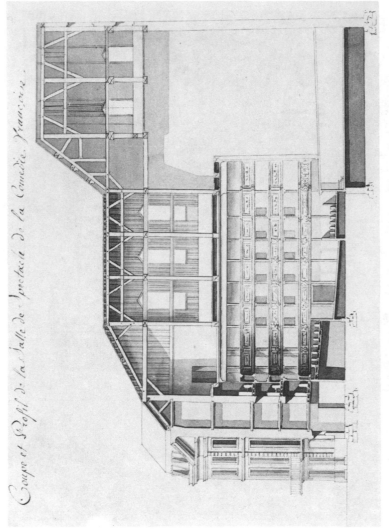

Coupe et Profil de la Salle de Spectacle de la Comédie Française.

Plate II. Comédie-Française playhouse, sectional design by François d'Orbay (ca. 1687)

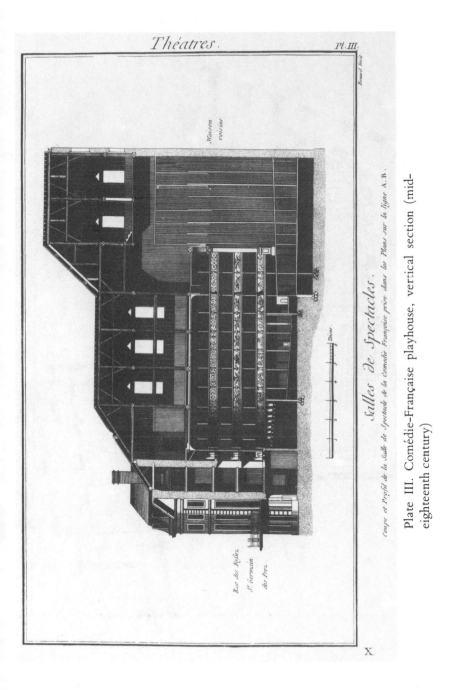

Salles de Spectacles.

Coupe et Profil de la Salle de Spectacle de la Comédie Françoise prise dans les Plans sur la ligne A.B.

Plate III. Comédie-Française playhouse, vertical section (mid-eighteenth century)

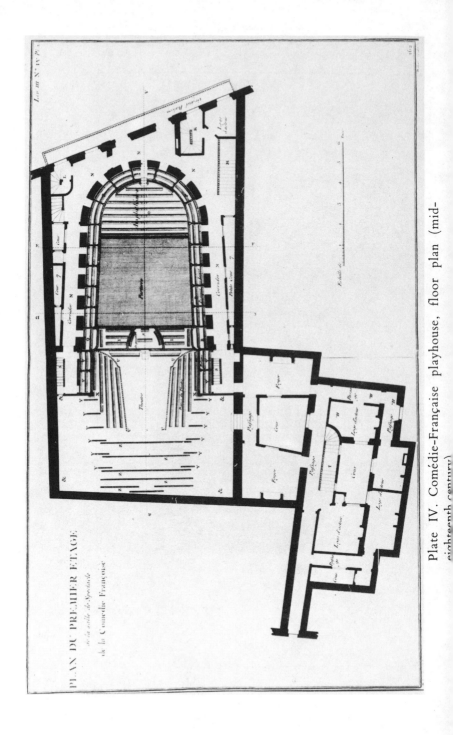

Plate IV. Comédie-Française playhouse, floor plan (mid-
eighteenth century)

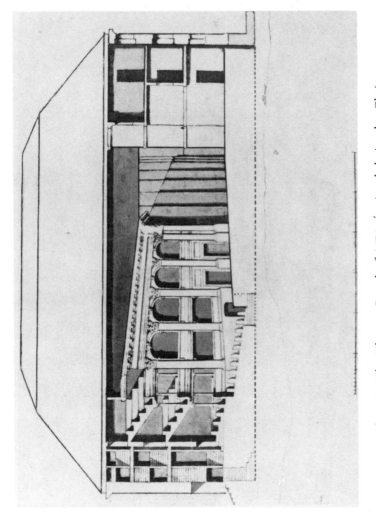

Plate V. The Theatre-Royal of 1674, 'sectional design by Christopher Wren

Chapter 2

"WIT, BE MY FACULTY": MANNERS COMEDY

"La question fonadmentale que pose le texte de théâtre est celle de son inscription dans le temps."[1] Ubersfeld's assertion holds for all drama, even the theater of the absurd, where time may be indeterminate or circular. Manners comedy, as we have seen, places the spectator in his own era, a historical time conveyed by textual allusion, scenic design, and costume. Specific historical events may be mentioned, as the "troubles" of the *Fronde* in *Tartuffe* (v. 181), or prevailing fashions in literature or life style in general (e.g., *préciosité*). The stage itself will convey visually a familiar, contemporary setting. Details of dress are of special importance in encoding a notion of the present. The modish may be contrasted with the dated: in *L'Ecole des maris* and *L'Avare*, tastefully fashionable clothing worn by characters who win our adherence is scoffed at by ludicrously arch-conservative personages like Sganarelle and Harpagon, enamored of their old-fashioned collar ruffs.

Space cooperates with time in situating drama, and in manners comedy the décor has a clear referent in external reality. In the Restoration comedies under study, not only are the fashionable haunts of the capital frequently mentioned but the setting itself moves constantly from one locale to another in a characteristic spatial flow. Thus the action of *The Way of the World* begins in a chocolate house, shifts to another public place, the modish St. James' Park, thence to a private space, Lady Wishfort's home. Other comedies present a similar mixture of private and public

space with perhaps yet more of the latter: allusions abound to
Hyde Park, the New Exchange, the Mulberry Garden, and other
gathering places favored by the happy few.

The image of Paris in Molière's comedies is less specific and
fluid. As we noted in the preceding chapter, Molière's settings are
usually fixed for the whole play and take the form either of a
conventional street scene or a room in a private house. Molière
tended to prefer the latter in his Paris comedies of manners. Only
Sganarelle, Les Fâcheux, L'Ecole des femmes, and *Monsieur de Pourceaugnac* take place in a "maisons et rues" décor; the action of the remaining comedies, including such repertory favorites as *Tartuffe,
Le Misanthrope, Le Bourgeois gentilhomme*, and *Le Malade imaginaire*,
unfolds in a private setting. Even this limited embodiment of space
can, however, convey a sense of topicality from such indicators as
interior decoration, furniture, and props.

One might assume that Molière, limited as he generally was to
one set of visual indices in a fixed setting, would by compensation
multiply allusions in the text to the fashionable topography of his
Paris. In *Les Fâcheux* he does mention such stylish thoroughfares as
Cours-la-Reine (v. 76), Le Mail, the Luxembourg Gardens, and
Les Tuileries (v. 691), but such precise verbal indicators are in fact
rare in his theater. The only other significant textual allusion is
that to La Place Royale in *La Critique de l'Ecole des femmes* (scene 1).
One may conclude that Molière saw no need to reinforce the impression of contemporary time and place beyond the global evidence of the plays themselves. The overall image of Paris life in
Tartuffe, Le Misanthrope, or *L'Avare*, for instance, is persuasive
enough to convince any spectator that he is seeing an aspect of his
own world.[2]

So far we have hardly advanced beyond the criterion of "realism" implicit in *la comédie de moeurs*. By indicating the topography
of Paris or London, by documenting familiar visual signs relating
to dress and setting, the comic playwright alludes specifically to
the mores of his time. But the realism of comedy, as we have already noted, tends inevitably toward distortion and caricature.

The propriety and distinction consonant with the world of the happy few exists often by implication only, and what we behold on stage is the parade of fools and knaves that contaminate refined life and convey by negative example an unrealized and perhaps unattainable ideal.

In an era that viewed man as corrupt in his essence, it was natural to depict that corruption in the outward manifestations of his inner nature. When Molière assigns to comedy the task of depicting "tous les défauts des hommes et principalement des hommes de notre siècle" (L'Impromptu de Versailles, scene 4), he gives expression to this image of eternal man eternally actualizing his folly. This castigat ridendo mores dimension of comedy afforded, incidentally, a helpful defense against the antitheatrical prejudice that was no less fanatical and unrelenting in France than in England; Prynne and Collier had their counterparts in Bossuet and Conti.[3] Defenders of the genre on both sides of the Channel repeatedly urged in rebuttal that comedy's chastising mission could instill a kind of moral awareness in the spectator that would make him a more enlightened and virtuous citizen.

Consequently the traditional point of reference for the genre was primarily ethical. If we denounce hypocrisy in Tartuffe or affectation in the courtiers of Le Misanthrope, we uphold by implication a standard of sincerity and authenticity. To ridicule self-blindness in such characters as Arnolphe or Orgon is to endorse tacitly that quintessential adage of humanistic wisdom "Know thyself." Thus satire viewed from a moral standpoint pinpoints breaches in a specific ethical code. To be comically effective, however, the message must be conveyed negatively; for to state within the text that truthfulness, integrity, and self-knowledge are universal goods is to moralize, and to present characters embodying such virtues is to edulcorate comedy. This tendency, already lurking in Molière's pontificating raisonneurs and idealized lovers, will develop into the sentimental comedy that will bulk large in both France and England during the next century.

Molière's own notions of comedy reflect, quite naturally, the ethical and corrective values attributed to the genre by neoclassical theorists. For scholars holding to the traditional position that an author's own intentions were fully adequate to interpret his work, no further conceptual probing was required. Thus may be explained perhaps the extraordinary tenacity of ethical comic theory in French scholarship and the reluctance of critics to relate Molière to a specifically social code as well. *Le Misanthrope* can be seen, of course, as a celebration of an absolute virtue like sincerity; but the play owes its hold upon the spectators to the problematics of interpersonal relationships, of social behavior, which it explores so relentlessly. Such concerns, though not the explicit purview of comedy, were certainly central to the social perspective of a moralist like La Rochefoucauld. After acknowledging that "on se préfère toujours," he implies a power of the will to civilize this egoism even if it cannot be eradicated: "Il faudrait cacher ce désir de préférence, puisqu'il est trop naturel en nous pour nous en pouvoir défaire; il faudrait faire son plaisir de celui des autres, ménager leur amour-propre, et ne le blesser jamais."[4] Similarly, in polite discourse one must hide one's natural desire to speak much and listen little, and cooperate in a genteel truce: "Il faut écouter ceux qui parlent, si on en veut être écouté."[5] Thus the concept of civility stood in a dynamic, compensatory relationship to the *amour-propre* that moralists saw everywhere rampant. A proper socializing process could smooth out the rough edges of the natural human shape, take the raw, aggressive, self-centered creature and make him into a polished man of the world. That these bedrock ideas could find expression in comedy is perfectly logical, especially since the positive representation of social excellence does not carry the same hazards as the depiction or codification of virtuous conduct in comedy. Whereas moralizing deflates the power of comedy, the example of the civil man or woman can only enhance and refine it. Civility in society carries with it a special grace born of wit, charm, urbanity; the *badinage* of a truly social man or woman is inherently comic in the best sense of the word.

To be convinced of this, we have only to note that in comedy, generally speaking, we prefer wit to virtue, style to sagacity.

The idea that comedy can depict a positive as well as negative image of social procedure, one that has had a long history in English scholarship, is central to the specifically Anglo-Saxon notion of the comedy of manners. Although the "manners" label itself dates only from the last century, the basic idea goes back to the Restoration. Congreve's much-quoted definition of the word *manner* is a good starting point: "Some distinguishing quality as for example, the Belair or Brillant of Mr. Brisk . . . or something of his own, that should look a little Jene-scay-quosh." (*The Double Dealer*, 2. 1). Less a definition than a series of suggestive hints, Congreve's phrase bears eloquent witness to the very elusiveness of the notion. On the one hand, we note the need for a highly idiosyncratic personal quality that draws admiring attention to the individual. Yet such attributes must find their place among social norms implied but not codified: "belair," "brillant." Individual style, though all-important, must yet conform to a general, socially accepted notion of gentility quite distinct from the iconoclastic separateness of an outsider like Alceste. As Peter Holland so aptly puts it: "There is a correct way of being witty, of talking with a masked lady, of conducting an affair, and that way is not merely a bookish repetition of another's brilliance but an individual's originality combined with a knowledge of the limits of social procedure" (p. 58).

The word *manner* carried as well a more traditional meaning, roughly equivalent to the French *moeurs* or *caractères* and similarly derived from the Aristotelian concept of *ethos* or *mores*—the distinguishing traits that enable us to classify and type all of humanity. In Restoration comedy the very names convey the image of a dominant tendency or impulse that makes the individual recognizable as a member of a class: Mr. Courtall, like Mr. Mirabell, is a gallant for all occasions; Sir Fopling Flutter is the archetypal social pretender; Lady Wishfort is the libidinous coquette—and so forth.

Molière's names conform to another tradition—fanciful ones vaguely suggestive of the pastoral (Cléante), the *commedia* (Valère, Angélique), or farce (Orgon, Argan); but it is clear that his audience was well aware of underlying character types. *La Lettre sur le Misanthrope*, a spirited defense of Molière's play by the dramatist himself or an admirer, never mentions the names of the chief personages. They are identified only as "la coquette" (Célimène), "la prude" (Arsinoé), "un homme sage" (Philinte), and "le misanthrope" (Alceste).[6] Boileau shows the same taxonomic turn of mind when he admonishes would-be authors of comedy to learn the art of portraying such varied types of humankind as "un Prodigue, un Avare / Un Honnête homme, un Fat, un Jaloux, un Bizarre."[7]

Although classificatory tags constitute an important aspect of manners theory, the *comedy* of manners clearly transcends this limited perspective to encompass something more far-reaching. In this regard, the implications of the Congreve quotation bear careful pondering. To begin with, *manners* suggests admirable personal traits that make a character pleasant company, traits admittedly so impalpable that Congreve resigns himself to the defeatist "je ne sais quoi." It also conveys an idea of collective behavior: manners that, when good, affirm one's rightful membership in a dominant group and that, when bad, entail some kind of ostracism. Further, bad manners can signify not only antisocial behavior but imperfect or misguided attempts to display good manners. In comedy this dichotomy will necessarily arouse two kinds of laughter: mirthful complicity with those who embody exemplary social conduct, and derision directed at those who fail to meet proper standards.

We make distinctions between proper and defective social procedure by means of articles of faith implicit in our social code. In the highly ritualized and hierarchical society that characterized the elite of both London and Paris, a complex, multilevel system of signs existed by which each social stratum could be defined and recognized. Such diverse facets of behavior as dress, language, taste in culture, the social circles in which one moved, combined to

authenticate one's rightful place. The manners celebrated in Restoration comedy are precisely those that set the tone of upper-class
society. Whence the dominant characteristic already noted: the
perspective of all society is from the top; peasants, artisans,
burghers are judged by the standards of a refined, self-centered
clique projecting its Town and Court values upon the entire
country.

Across the Channel we encounter the same elitist mentality.
Boileau clearly envisaged genteel comedy as his ideal. The conduct to be imitated by the genre is that of the highest classes: "Etudiez la Cour, et connaissez la Ville. / L'une et l'autre est toujours
en modèles fertile" (p. 178). Theirs as well is the diction to be
recorded in comic discourse. The difficulty of so doing Boileau
conveys by a remarkable oxymoron: "Il faut que ses acteurs (i.e.,
of comedy) badinent noblement" (ibid.). The verb belongs to
comedy, the adverb to the tragic genre: *badinage*—refined, spirited
banter—must eschew facile, coarse effects and also rise without
solemnity to the highest decorum. To be mirthful in good taste is a
problem that Molière himself emphasized in *La Critique de l'Ecole des
femmes*, scene 6: "C'est une étrange entreprise que celle de faire
rire les honnêtes gens"—discriminating people of refinement less
predisposed, perhaps, to spontaneous jocularity than the "wits"
across the Channel. And we recall Boileau's harsh condemnation
of Molière's lapses from taste, his betrayal of "l'agréable et le fin"
(ibid.) for the vulgar slapstick of *Les Fourberies de Scapin*.

To give this social code concrete substance, both Restoration
comedy and Molière's plays abound with allusions to contemporary mores. As concerns the Frenchman, Gaines has isolated seven
groups of "social indicators"—money, offices, clothing, servants,
houses and land, transportation, and language—by which these
indices can be described and quantified. His justification of this
method reaffirms the value of the manners approach in general:
"Lest these factors be dismissed as merely picturesque, superficial
effects, it should be remembered that the ability to notice outward
appearances and to distinguish between them was vital to Euro-

peans in the seventeenth century, when each social body had its
place in a hierarchy of possessions, uniforms, and behavior" (p.
19). It is worth repeating that the comedy under review here does
not present these indices with a sociological objectivity that gives
all class attributes the same intrinsic value. The signs that distinguish the lower elements in the hierarchy are interpreted through
those characterizing the highest echelons. Middle-class manners
bring derision, whether for the London "citizen" or the Paris *bon
bourgeois*. The lower classes—peasants, workers—appear as rough
of speech, coarse in manners; the servants of comedy, whatever
their refreshing impertinence and their folk wisdom, have no class
identity of their own and belong to the ideological world of their
masters.

It is beyond the scope of this study to catalogue in any systematic way so complex a social code as that which actualizes
manners comedy in the seventeenth century. No set of sign groups
can be exhaustive, and the problem of perspective—of one complex of indicators observed through another—clouds the issue
further. There is, however, one aspect of social conduct that, although impossible to quantify, affirms an all-embracing social
ideal appropriate to embodiment in comedy: wit. Indeed, such is
the significance of wit in Restoration comedy that a respected
scholar, we recall, has made a persuasive case for abandoning the
word *manners* and rebaptizing the whole category "The Restoration Comedy of Wit," the title of Fujimura's 1952 book.

Wit may appear today as a slender support for a whole comic
tradition. Modern usage has limited what was once a many-
faceted concept. Naturally, the ability to be witty in the modern
sense—to invent *bons mots* on the spur of the moment, to shine by
word play—was as highly prized then as now. The much-quoted
anecdote concerning Buckingham's intervention at a performance
of a Dryden play is a good case in point. When an actress paused
during a memory lapse after declaiming "My wound is great, because it is so small," Buckingham is said to have completed the
couplet spontaneously from the audience: "Then 'twould be

greater were it none at all." Though almost certainly apocryphal,[8] the story illustrated the high esteem accorded to instant verbal inventiveness. The banter, the epigrammatic exchanges, the verbal sparring that characterizes Restoration dialogue is the dramatized form of this quality. Congreve gave exuberant expression to the carefree spirit, the *joie de vivre* implicit in the word with his wit's creed: "Come, come, leave business to idlers and wisdom to fools; they have need of them; wit, be my faculty, and pleasure my occupation and let father time shake his glass" (*The Old Bachelor*, 1.1).

Yet, in Restoration comedy, wit is more than witticism. For Fujimura it is an "intellectual and esthetic ideal" linked to the notion of decorum, propriety. "Decorum," he writes, "was never an artificial code of manners, nor a mere matter of riband [sic] and fine talk and elegant manners. It was a vital ideal, a standard of thought and conduct to which the intelligent and cultivated person aspired, and it implied not only intellectual discrimination, elegance and sound judgment, but naturalness." And he concludes: "Decorum (true wit) might be defined simply as natural elegance of thought and conduct, based on respect for sound judgment, fidelity to nature and a due regard for beauty" (p. 27).

Fujimura is certainly correct in giving such a wide orbit to the term. When Restoration characters say, "He/She has wit," they refer to a composite of qualities transcending the mere ability to banter or the unregenerate hedonism voiced by Congreve. In one terse syllable, they express a general refinement and social charm that permeates all aspects of collective life. Indeed, Fujimura, in my view, over-intellectualizes wit and dissociates it unduly from the social sphere. After all, naturalness—a distinctive aspect of wit in Fujimura's view—is far from an absolute quality. It is an arbitrary social category subject to the same conventions and vicissitudes as any mode of behavior; what is felt to be natural at one moment—a given vestimentary fashion, for instance, or a manner of speaking—may appear to be absurdly affected at another. More significantly, wit, however inward it may be, can be manifested

and validated only in a social context. The closet wit is a contradiction in terms.

Because such notions as natural behavior are relative and basically arbitrary, the line between acceptable wit and breaches of it
will always be difficult to delineate in society. Elegant banter may
shade into raillery, teasing repartee that can go to embarrassing
lengths. *Médisance* is not far away, for wit can always be at another's expense; a few notches further down, we reach outright character assassination. As well, the contrived nature of all wit poses
other problems. At what point is an intricate play on words a sign
of wit or an insufferable affectation? We are never very far from
culture-specific criteria.

Yet the fact that we are dealing with comedy, with a theatrical
representation of wit, alleviates some of these difficulties. Comedy
traditionally presents strong contrasts, partly because they have
comic value, partly because they help clarify the informing vision.
Indicators that in real society might present ambiguities are sim-
plified and caricatured to the point that no misunderstanding is
possible. A very strong line is traced between what is approved of
as natural grace and what is mocked as affected or boorish behavior. The tendency to make characters a single-minded embodiment of one moral trait furthers this schematization process. Costume may underline character polarities: ludicrously exaggerated
attire makes fashionable dress, even with its ostentation, simple
and tasteful by comparison. Acting styles too may reinforce this
contrast. As Peter Holland tells us, the principals of Restoration
comedy played their roles without undue emphasis, adopting as
much as possible the easy diction of the drawing room; the fops and
bumpkins, on the contrary, distorted norms of polite speech to the
point of caricature (p. 59).

In all probability, then, the Restoration audience had no trou-
ble differentiating between true wit and false, and the dialectical
opposition between the two must have been apparent at all times.
This characteristic polarity is well summarized by Kathleen

Lynch: "The social game calls for an intellectual equipment in which certain characters are manifestly deficient. These characters are intruders on the social scene. . . . A marked contrast to such a personage is presented by the fully initiated members of the social group, who comply intelligently with its unwritten laws" (p. 37).

A basic dialectic of inclusion/exclusion obtains from these contrasting groups. Those who live up to the behavioral standards of the initiate constitute the happy few. Characters unable or unwilling to abide by proper social procedure are found wanting. They may not be literally excluded—the pretenders gravitate compulsively to the circles they wish to penetrate—but the audience perceives them through the condescending gaze of their social betters.

The interaction of these groups defines what for Fujimura is the structure of the "comedy of wit": "The plot consists of an outwitting situation involving Truewits, Witwouds and Witlesses" (p. 65). The latter two groups function as foils for the Truewit, the ones being mere "pretenders to wit" (p. 69), the others loutish blockheads for whom genteel manners are a closed book. Fujimura points out the striking resemblance of this threefold grouping with the triad in Aristotle's *Nicomachean Ethics* where the witty person is the middle term between the buffoon and the boor. The degree to which Aristotle's distinctions anticipate the structuring principle of Restoration comedy is indeed noteworthy, for the philosopher, notwithstanding his ethical turn of mind, is thinking here of social criteria: "People whose fun is in good taste are called witty. . . . The characteristic of [this] mean state is tact. A person of tact is one who will use and listen to such language as is suitable to any honorable gentlemen" (quoted by Fujimura, p. 24). Social sensitivity, then, is the true mark of wit. The buffoon lacks this awareness of the *à propos*: "a slave to his own sense of humour" (ibid.), he is concerned only with eliciting laughter and often does so in bad taste or at the wrong time. The boor has no social value whatsoever: "He contributes nothing and takes offense at everything" (ibid.); graceless and ill-humored, he stands radically apart from his fellows.

To pass now to some generalizations about these character types as they appear in Restoration comedy: truewits are members of the Town, the fashionable part of London, free from contamination from the mercantile City toward the east. They are "gentlemen" and "gentlewomen" for the most part, people of "quality" (that is, members of the aristocracy, although actual titles are seldom mentioned). Their opulence frees them from the need for remunerated endeavor, allows them to enjoy unabashedly and unremittingly the genteel amusements of their lofty clan. They thrive in the reflected light of the Circle, the king's entourage, and, with the alliance of the great families of the realm, constitute a composite center of taste comparable in France to "la Cour et la Ville."

For those who take a strictly moral view of comedy, the problem with truewits, especially the young gallants, is that their taste may be exemplary and their life stylish but their conduct reprehensible. They pile up amorous intrigues and take equal pleasure in forming and breaking love affairs. City husbands are always fair game for them; to produce cuckolds is to wear a badge of honor as flattering as the horns themselves are loathsome. They come out with cynical and rakish epigrams to mock conventional morality with happy abandon, especially the institution of marriage. In short, nothing is taken seriously, a point that for some critics defines the "code of the times."[9] It is important, however, to put this amorality in a more positive perspective. Cynicism, to begin with, is a protection against pomposity and unseemly sentimentality— two elements that, more than any other, inhibit the full-blown *vis comica.* Moreover, the world of comedy in all the history of the genre tends to contrast not virtue and vice but cleverness and stupidity. The animal fable is never far away: the cunning of the fox and his smug tone of triumph are justified by the vanity and ugliness of the crow. To expect the fox to be sincere and upright in a world of fools is to expect the impossible, and the Restoration had no illusions about the law of the jungle in its lofty world. Even though society could be made more pleasant by respect for civilized behavior, man's basic egoism, as mercilessly exposed in England by Hobbes as it was in France by Pascal and La Rochefoucauld, lurked in the background of all social intercourse. Restoration comedy accepted mankind's self-serving nature and faced it with the same blend of lucidity, tolerance, and saving cynicism as we find in La Rochefoucauld's social view.

Besides embodying a certain life-style, the truewits have an additional function then of exposing the hypocrisy of society, of stripping away appearances to expose the naked mechanisms of human nature. Their mode of living makes them appreciate civilized behavior, and their lucidity prompts them to reveal the animal underneath. In this respect, there is a considerable gamut in Restoration comedy between the flaying satire found in Wycherley— no one can forget the commentary on society that Horner makes by word and deed in *The Country Wife*—and Congreve's more tolerant bent.

Truewit depiction often takes two human forms in Restoration comedy. The fashionable young gallant rarely functions alone; he usually consorts with at least one like-minded companion with whom he can boast of his conquests, to whom he can confide his next amorous moves, whom he can make a partner in a duet of cynical epigrams. Thus Dorimant and Medley in *The Man of Mode*, Valentine and Scandal, Mirabell and Fainall in Congreve's *Love for Love* and *The Way of the World*, respectively. Equally characteristic is the "pair of witty lovers," to use Nicoll's phrase, "the woman as emancipated as the man, their dialogue free and graceful, an air of refined cynicism over the whole production" (p. 185). The Restoration did not invent the "gay couple," to use the title of the authoritative book on the subject,[10] although Dryden did much to popularize a courtship joust that went back to Elizabethan times.

The "merry war of wits" between, for example, Beatrice and Benedick of Shakespeare's *Much Ado About Nothing* charms us still today.

Not infrequently a pair of men is matched with two "gentle-women," and the resulting foursome gives the play its principal plot impetus. Thus Ariana and Gatty stand opposite Courtall and Freeman in Etherege's *She Would if She Could*; Emelia and Harriet are courted by Dorimant and Medley in *The Man of Mode*. Such plays usually close with two impending marriages, concluded after much sarcasm on the subject. Sometimes one of the two ladies is already married, as in Vanbrugh's *The Provok'd Wife*; Heartfree woos and wins Bellinda, and we presume Constant to be successful in providing Lady Brute better entertainment than her loutish and debauched husband.

To pass now to the opposite, non-exemplary pole of the dialec-tic: a first false wit group aspires to the truewit world but lacks the discretion and judgment to assimilate an intricate and subtle social code. It represents the subtypes of the fop, or coxcomb; Sir Fopling Flutter in *The Man of Mode*, that consummate Gallophile popinjay, is a memorable embodiment of the type, as well as Witwoud and Petulant of *The Way of the World*, the irrepressible buffoons who outdo themselves in contrived similitudes and inept wooing. Such characters reinforce the comic mood because they often have a buoyant, entertaining nature; they wish to be at one with polite society, and they are ludicrous only because, in their homage to genteel ways, they are incapable of refined judgment. But members of a second category scorn the social game itself, whose intricacies they find absurd. Here are the outsiders of comedy. The country bumpkin belongs to this group, and Congreve gives us a good example in Sir Wilfull of *The Way of the World*. He arrives in fashionable London in his riding costume, wears his boots in the best salons, and will have none of the courtly habits of his half-brother Witwoud. He is content to leave the capital and resume his simple country routine. This outsider is rather winning in his rustic simplicity, but a more typical one, the outright boor, shows the contrast more starkly between civilized and churlish conduct. No better example can be found among the Restoration masterpieces than Sir John Brute, the aptly named husband of *The Provok'd Wife*. Here Vanbrugh gives us a powerful antisocial portrait of a foul-mouthed knight given to drunkenness, blasphemy, sadism, and debauchery in general. Such figures belong to the *pharmakos* archetype where society takes its revenge on nonconformist conduct by humiliation and exclusion. The embittered, vain misanthropist of Shakespeare's *Twelfth Night*, Malvolio, is in this lineage. A more whimsical brother, the Jacques of *As You Like It*, summarizes pithily in his last words the repugnance the outsider feels about a frivolous society: "So to your pleasures; / I am for other than dancing measures" (4. 4).

A special recurring type, more difficult to place in the truewit triad, deserves a fuller discussion. Almost every manners masterpiece depicts a version of the superannuated coquette. Among the most noteworthy are: Lady Cockwood (*She Would if She Could*), Mrs. Loveit (*The Man of Mode*), Lady Fidget (*The Country Wife*), Lady Wishfort (*The Way of the World*), and Lady Fancifull (*The Provok'd Wife*). As so many of these names imply, this type is driven by strong sexual impulses that incline her to grossness and promiscuity. As she is almost always married and beyond the age of effective competition with the young, her lust is ludicrous both by degree and circumstance. Her vulnerability heightens her vanity, making her easy prey for deceitful courtship by the gallants; jealousy is her curse, for she is almost always cruelly jilted. Not infrequently she hides her lubricious nature behind a veil of propriety that shades into prudishness. Much comic value obtains from her preoccupation with "reputation," "forms," "decorums." Her jealousy and affected delicacy of principle incite her to backbiting and carping criticism of others.

Her lack of propriety and self-knowledge place her clearly among the false wits, but in an ambiguous relationship to the witwoud/witless dichotomy. She aspires to the courtship rituals and privileges that are an essential part of genteel living; she attempts

witty speech but weighs it down with the kind of affectation typical of the fop. Witness Lady Wishfort's admonition to a suitor:
"You must not attribute my yielding to any sinister appetite, or
indigestion of Widow-hood; nor impute my complacency to any
lethargy of continence. I hope you do not think me prone to any
Iteration of Nuptuals" (4. 1). Such talk makes her a witwoud. But
her censoriousness, her spiteful envy of the young and beautiful
make her akin to the boor, whose essence is to be hostile to the
mood of fun and festivity.

In any event, such types have obviously no place among truewits. Being married to a titled husband (one notes the number of
"Ladies") confers no special priviledge, for rank alone does not
carry the holder to a place among the elect. Country knights like
Sir Wilfull Witwoud, a London knight like Sir John Brute and his
aristocratic drinking and whoring companions Lord Rake and Colonel Bully—such dubious aristocrats draw no respect from the
spectator. As was the case with the foolish *marquis* in Molière's
theater, the mores of the time obviously allowed for an unflattering portraiture of at least a segment of the upper classes.

Although somewhat schematic, the threefold pattern of characterization just described does help bring to the fore the social
vision that appears to be inherent in manners comedy: a hierarchical concept not rigidly tied to rank—or to moral traits—but rather
to a distinction and refinement usually associated with rank but
not always in conformity with conventional morality.

Can this schema be applied profitably to Molière? In Molière's
time the same significance was attached to "La Cour et La Ville"
as we find in the London of the Restoration with its dominant
Court and Town. The derision projected upon the *bon bourgeois*
parallels the contempt in which London "citizens" were held.
As we noted earlier, Molière's theater is generally accepted now
as reflecting this elitist, hierarchical social structure: to quote Bénichou, "les figures, et plus généralement la manière d'être, aux-
quelles Molière a attaché l'agrément et la sympathie répondent

sans conteste à une vue noble de la vie" (pp. 159-60). If this is the case, his plays can be appropriately analyzed along the lines of the character patterns we find across the Channel. Accordingly, we shall examine the truewit aspects of Molière's theater in the following chapter, after which the witwouds—Molière's pretenders—and the witless—the antisocial outsiders—will be studied in separate sections.

Chapter 3

"L'Esprit du monde": Truewits in Molière

Upbraided by his wife for his social pretentions, Monsieur Jourdain, Molière's bourgeois gentilhomme, expresses his aspirations in these terms: "Je veux avoir de l'esprit et savoir raisonner parmi les honnêtes gens" (3. 3). His phrase, though comic coming from him, neatly encapsulates a French equivalent of the cluster of ideas explored in the preceding chapter concerning manners comedy in Restoration England. First, we infer the acknowledged presence of an arbitrating group, an elite repository of taste and tact not unlike the cultivated people of the Town: "les honnêtes gens." Membership in this cultivated circle is validated by exemplary conversation: *raisonner* here evokes the spirited give-and-take of salon discourse, not the deductive logic sometimes implied by the related word *raisonnement*. Finally, the faculty that enables the would-be salon habitué to shine in polite conversation is identified by the word *esprit*. Although the term in seventeenth-century France had a wide range of meanings—religious, philosophical, and social—it is clear from the context that *esprit* can be usefully linked to the all-important notion of wit in the Restoration. Like the English word, it carried a broad range of purely social connotations. Jourdain may be thinking only of the clever repartee that he subsequently counterfeits so lamentably in the banquet scene with his *belle marquise* (4. 1). Verbal inventiveness was, of course, highly prized in seventeenth-century France, not only in the spontaneous *saillies spirituelles* appropriate to the salon world but also in what were known as "ouvrages de l'esprit," constructions not of the material world but wrought out of words. Thus Louis XIV's laconic judgment of Racine, as reported by Madame de Sévigné after a court performance of *Esther* (letter of 21 February 1689), is actually a high compliment: "Racine a bien de l'esprit."

More germane to our purpose, however, is the wider relevance of the term. *Esprit* carried with it similar values of interpersonal tact, social grace, entertaining *entregent* implied in the Restoration compliment "he has wit." The quotation heading this chapter, taken from *Les Femmes savantes* (v. 1346), confirms the comparison. "L'esprit du monde" summarizes the ideal of decorum practiced by the *honnête homme*, a code of social discrimination and *agrément* offered as an antidote to the learned pomposity and narcissism of Philaminte's embryonic "académie." In his wide-ranging discussion of "worldliness," Peter Brooks formulates an expression of ultimate social aptitude perfectly consonant with the social ideal of manners comedy: "a style of urbane, unpretentious wit, the unpedantic, elegant, nonspecialized exploration of serious subjects of interest to all cultivated ladies and gentlemen."[1]

This cultural code was no less arbitrary and relative in France than it was in England. As in our own day, fashions evolved with greater or lesser speed; what was accepted as tasteful and natural at one moment became quaint and faintly ridiculous to a later generation. This fact is especially evident in the historical evolution of the *mot d'esprit*. A witticism always betrays some degree of *recherche*; the unexpected analogy of the Restoration epigram, a clever metaphorical association, a pun or *calembour*, all show a verbal imagination at work. The contrived nature of such devices can either be masked by cultural acceptance or exposed as absurdly labored. A good case in point is Boileau's well-known mockery of an equally famous Théophile de Viau image. To say of a blood-stained sword that it blushes with shame—"il en rougit, le traître!"—smacks of the ludicrous at a later time. A far better example of wit, in Boileau's opinion, is a king's expression of high-minded forgiveness for wrongs done to him while he was a lesser person: "Un roi de France ne venge point les injures d'un Duc d'Orléans."[2] Yet from our standpoint, we note merely a distaste for the bold metaphorical expression characteristic of an earlier poetic tradition and a preference for a tamer form of metonymy more typical of full-blown classicism.

The basically contrived nature of the *bon mot* leads to the same ambiguity in France with *esprit* as we noted in England with wit. So readily is wit counterfeited that the word itself can acquire a pejorative ring; similarly in France *esprit* merges into the ironic formula *bel-esprit* with its nuance of display and affectation. For example, Mascarille, the would-be fop of *Les Précieuses ridicules*, claims to arise regularly surrounded by "une demi douzaine de beaux esprits" and promises to establish "une académie de beaux esprits" right in the précieuses' drawing room (scene 9). Thus a positive adjective is needed to put an end to such ambivalence. Wit is "true," *l'esprit* is *véritable*. Even if in retrospect this sense of a permanent norm turns out, like all such intimations of immortality, to be illusory, it does help us acquire the historical perspective necessary to interpret Molière's social message with some degree of assurance. Fortunately, we are helped by the tendency of comedy itself to fall into strong polarities with extremes of caricature and idealization.

We may proceed, then, with the assumption that there is in Molière a group of characters who may be loosely labeled "truewits," people who embody *l'esprit véritable* required to function properly in elevated society. Because we are in a hierarchical world, we expect, to begin with, some indicators that relate to social class, to rank. As moral (and presumably social) excellence was assumed as a general principle to be directly proportionate to one's place on the ladder—an article of faith that justified the stratified distribution of power and influence—we might infer that the truewits would be high on the social scale. There are no princes or dukes in Molière's *comédies de moeurs*—characters of such exalted rank belong to a more "heroic" genre like his courtly *divertissements*—but the lower titles are indeed represented. Dorante, "le grand seigneur éclairé" of *Le Bourgeois gentilhomme*, is a *comte*, and his lady Dorimène enjoys the rank of *marquise*. The well-mannered courtier who intrudes into George Dandin's world is a notch below Dorante in his status as *vicomte*, a rank also held by the Cléante of *La Comtesse d'Escarbagnas*. Another Dorante, that of *La Critique de l'Ecole des femmes*, holds membership in the lowest noble order, that of *chevalier*. But not all titled personages in Molière embody social distinction. Indeed, his greatest scorn was reserved for members of the order that stood directly under the dukedom and above that of *comte*, the *marquis*. Whereas Restoration playwrights mocked country and London knights and their ridiculous "ladies"—the knight being on the same level as the *chevalier*—Molière singled out a relatively high rank from which to draw his new figure of fun, his new "plaisant de la comédie" replacing the "valet bouffon" of past times (*L'Impromptu de Versailles*, scene 2). The airtight compartments, the rigid hierarchization of feudal times had come to exist only vestigially, sapped of their genuine value. Class boundaries were eroding, and a proliferation of noble titles bestowed by the king further cheapened the significance of rank. Such fops as Acaste and Clitandre and the ludicrous nobleman of *La Critique*, all *marquis*, carry no sense of a superior order at all.

In fact, as with Restoration comedy, aristocratic title in Molière's comedies is not often indicated. Instead we have a vague impression of people of quality belonging more to an overall gentry than to a specific order. Their claim to distinction is validated more by a style of life than a named rank. This somewhat blurred picture reflects the fluid realities of history in Molière's time. The rise of mercantilism and the subjugation of the warrior class by an ever more centralized monarchy gave double impetus to profound changes. Alongside the old nobility of ancient families—the *gentilhommerie* and the more recent but respectable *noblesse de robe*—arose a kind of instant aristocracy composed largely of lesser folk ennobled by royal decree. The system of *charges*, or purchased offices, provided for a mutually advantageous exchange: the king filled his treasury with money acquired from the rising middle class and in return gave the *bourgeoisie* respectability by noble titles and privileges dispensed in profusion. Moralists like La Bruyère with a conservative view of society yearned for a return to the watertight compartments of feudalism and denounced bitterly the evils of unmerited wealth—*les biens de fortune*—that launched the valet's progress through various purchased functions and offices to spurious membership in the second order: "Sosie [the author's code name for the servant class] a de la livrée passé par une petite recette à une sous-ferme; et par les concussions, la violence, et l'abus qu'il a fait de ses *pouvoirs*, il s'est enfin, sur les ruines de plusieurs familles, élevé à quelque grade. Devenu noble par une charge, il ne lui manquait que d'être un homme de bien. Une place de marguillier [an honorific parish function] a fait ce prodige."[3] La Bruyère's anger and the dismay of the great noble families are understandable when one measures the degree to which the old distinctions were being flouted. As Gaines points out, some offices like that of *secrétaire d'état* carried instant hereditary nobility. Others conferred personal nobility on the holder and, when passed to the grandson, bestowed an inherited title on the lineage (pp. 6, 24). The author argues plausibly, for instance, that Orgon had inherited a *charge* from his father and that Damis, his own son, would therefore carry a hereditary title (p. 203).

This rising *tiers-état* had no common measure with the aggressively capitalist middle class that would emerge later and develop its own self-justifying ideology. So bent was the seventeenth-century financier or successful merchant on acquiring nobility that he not only immobilized his wealth in land—the first attribute of the gentry—but willingly relinquished vast sums to the crown in return for bubble titles. The first concern of the wealthy *bourgeois* was to obliterate any sign of low birth, to flee demeaning commercial activity, to acquire all appropriate signs of status—to live nobly, in a word.

Generally speaking, this is the *bourgeoisie* that Molière portrays in his theater. Except for Harpagon, who carries on his usury, the paterfamilias usually leads a life of opulence and leisure, even if in other respects he is at odds with social norms. Among the younger members of his family, we find the fashionable gallants and well-bred young ladies upon whom the love interest usually devolves. In the main, a thriving upper-class life is represented, where actual title is subordinate to appearance. Molière gives us, then, an appropriate image of a similarly ambiguous social reality.

It must not be assumed, however, that there was massive dislocation of the social order. The upward mobility of the middle class was carefully controlled. The *bourgeois* could become noble only after well-defined steps were patiently taken and validated by royal prerogative. Of special importance in the bid for rank were: exemption from the *taille* (the distinctive tax burden of commoners), purchase of land, alliances with great families by marriage (hypergamy), acquisition of important *charges*, and so on. To leap over these preconditions is to seize title, not earn it legitimately. As Gaines points out, an episode in *Le Bourgeois gentilhomme* illustrates perfectly this tension between the impatience of ambition and the all-too-plodding pace by which status could be obtained. Monsieur Jourdain yearns to jump in one lifetime from lowly cloth-selling to a dukedom. When he asks Cléonte if he is a "gentilhomme"—that is, if he belongs to the old *noblesse d'épée*—the young man's answer is hedged with caution: "Je suis né de parents, sans doute, qui ont tenu des charges honorables. Je me suis acquis dans les armes l'honneur de six ans de services, et je me trouve assez de bien pour tenir dans le monde un rang assez passable. Mais . . . je ne suis point gentilhomme" (3. 12). Cléonte's life illustrates admirably the lengthy, step-by-step movement toward *annoblissement*: his parents had already begun the process by acquiring an office with, probably, some kind of title; he himself had edged toward a warrior-class identity with his six years of military service; his fortune ("bien") is adequate to sustain a proper place in polite society ("le monde"). In short, he is well on his way but has not yet arrived, nor is he crass enough to hasten the process. Exemplary in his honesty, lucidity, and distinction, Cléonte is an emblematic truewit in Molière's theater, embodying upper-class values while admitting to his somewhat ambiguous social position.

Molière's image of "la ville" avoids, then, specific delineation of rank while suggesting at the same time a degree of sophistication, opulence, and carefree pleasure-seeking (among the young, at least) appropriate to the elite. In this the Frenchman resembles his English contemporaries. Specific rank is rarely mentioned in Restoration comedy (except for derogatory reference to knights); but the young are almost invariably "gentlemen" and "gentlewomen," that is, upper-class people of the Town.

As for the king's circle, or *la Cour*—the supreme authority on taste—manners comedy acknowledged its hegemony while keeping it at an appropriate distance. Tragedy is the purview of elevated rank and the decorum of high seriousness its proper theatrical appurtenance. Molière does take pains to underline the superior wisdom of the king and his entourage: "La grande épreuve de toutes vos comédies," as Dorante, Molière's spokesman, argues against the pedantic Lysidas in *La Critique de l'Ecole des femmes*, "c'est le jugement de la cour; . . . c'est son goût qu'il faut étudier pour trouver l'art de réussir" (scene 6). This praise shades into fulsomeness in Clitandre's defense of the Court in *Les Femmes savantes*: "Elle a du sens commun pour se connaître à tout" (v. 1344), he concludes after a lengthy eulogy. And the king's clairvoyance lifts the gloom from the fifth act of *Tartuffe* as his symbolic presence in the person of the Exempt brings order and justice. In general, the Court takes the image of a distant Providence, looking benignly down upon an elite eager to implement its tastes and values.

Although it is easy to say that norms are exemplified in manners comedy, the isolation and description of specific rules of social procedure present problems inherent in the comic genre. They may be after the fact summarized as precepts, but they cannot always be presented as such in the actual fabric of comedy. As we noted earlier, moralizing didacticism tends to dampen the good-humoured banter, the tasteful repartee that, more than ac-

tual substance, sets the exemplary tone. This is especially the case
for Restoration comedy, where truewits must affect airy cynicism
and an ironic, worldly-wise detachment. Molière tended more to
codify accepted standards of conduct, to give them the status of
aphorisms. From Ariste's pronouncements in *L'Ecole des maris* to
Cléante's eloquent speeches in *Tartuffe*, to the passionate, self-
righteous moralizing of Clitandre and Henriette in *Les Femmes savantes*, there is a serious disputatious strain in Molière's comedy,
even among exemplary characters.[4] Yet we must avoid, of course,
the long-accepted fallacy that wherever there is pronouncement
in Molière there is authorial wisdom. Molière often devalues precept, giving it comic associations with wrongheadedness, or pedantry, as with Alceste and Madame Jourdain, or the dogmatism
of the medical profession.

Truewit norms in Restoration comedy tend, we recall, to be
distinctively embodied in the courting couple. Molière's picture of
galanterie is quite different, although not without its own exemplariness. The romantic plot centering on young lovers was characteristic of Molière's dramaturgy, but nowhere do we find the "merry
war of wits," the clever jousting between gallant and lady characteristic of the Restoration; thus the good humor that sets the tone
in England and, often more than subject matter, conveys the comic
message is lacking in Molière. We are certainly meant to be sym-
pathetic to young love and to take its part against obstacle figures.
But courtship discourse in Molière is tinged with a certain sentimentality; marriage, instead of being the object of posturing cynicism, is defended with naïve eloquence even in a cerebral character like the Henriette of *Les Femmes savantes*:

> Et qu'est-ce qu'à mon âge on a de mieux à faire,
> Que d'attacher à soi, par le titre d'époux,
> Un homme qui vous aime et qui soit aimé de vous,
> Et de cette union, de tendresse suivie,
> Se faire les douceurs d'une innocente vie?
>
> [Vv. 20–24]

Molière does mitigate this sentimentality by a slightly parodic, affected inflection in his lovers' dialogue—a result, no doubt, of his *commedia dell'arte* discipleship and the typically contrived discourse of *innamorati*. The first scenes of *L'Avare*, for instance, are redolent with a certain *maniérisme* calculated to bring an indulgent smile to the spectator's face: "Hé quoi? charmante Elise, vous devenez mélancolique, après les obligeantes assurances que vous avez eu la bonté de me donner de votre foi?" (etc.)

In purely quantitative terms, however, Molière's lovers are much less prominent than the Restoration gallants who are usually the driving force of the action. Molière's *soupirants* lack the subtle combination of complicity and detachment required to form a spirited, ironic relationship with their ladies, and they seldom establish the kind of male bond that often unites two gallants in Restoration comedy.[5] But if Molière's young truewits have relatively little occasion to display their exemplariness in action and dialogue, there are other ways of suggesting to a spectator the sense of a presiding norm. The most elementary and immediate complex of indicators conveyed in theater is visual. What a character wears will tell us as much about what he will do and how we should react to him as what he may say. In the case of Molière, we are fortunate in having a fair amount of contemporary evidence about costuming in addition to what the text itself tells us. Several of his own costumes are described in some detail in the inventory of his personal effects after his death.[6] Engravings from printed editions of Molière's comedies are an especially precious source of information about what actors wore. Six individually published comedies carried a frontispiece, two of them engraved by Chauveau: *L'Ecole des maris, L'Amour médecin, L'Ecole des femmes, Le Misanthrope, Le Médecin malgré lui*, and *Tartuffe*. But the most important data of this kind are furnished by the set of engravings Brissart produced for the 1682 edition of Molière's complete works (see Appendix). Brissart used most of the six earlier engravings for his own inspiration, so that a comparison of the illustrations from the 1660s with that from up to twenty years later tells the historian much about changing vestimentary fashions. More significantly, Brissart continued the freeze-frame approach used by Chauveau. A given moment is captured and fixed as emblematic of the whole action. Thus, Orgon emerging from under the table to upbraid Tartuffe in act 4 (no. 20) and Arnolphe's lesson to Agnès in act 3 of L'Ecole des femmes (no. 8) were both obviously calculated to revive in the reader's memory all the events of the play. Consequently it may be assumed that this moment of stopped action had made the greatest impact on the theatergoer. Since there is an engraving for each of Molière's plays, even Dom Juan (although it was never restaged until the nineteenth century), we possess an invaluable composite image of what Molière meant to his own spectator.

What is striking in these representations is the frequency with which the young gallant is portrayed, even if, in the actual play, his role may be subordinate to others. A second salient feature of these many amoureux is their standardized costume. We see a fashionably dressed young man, sometimes with a plumed hat on his head or in his hand, always wearing a periwig, a fine, lace-trimmed justaucorps, or long coat, delicate high-heeled shoes accentuating a finely turned ankle, and, as an unmistakable emblem of upper-class rank, a sword often at his side (see nos. 1, 2, 4, 6, 7, 11, 14, 16, 18). In some of the scenes represented, we behold the gallant in a subservient attitude of obeisance to his lady (nos. 4, 6, 16) often under the nose of his rival or enemy. It is interesting to note in this regard that in a 1667 engraving depicting Le Médecin malgré lui the anonymous artist chose to represent, not the woodchopping Sganarelle depicted by Brissart (1, 5), but the gallant Léandre courting Lucinde while Sganarelle holds Géronte's attention (3, 6) (no. 15).

The presence of this fashionable courtier type in so many of these representations must correspond to a clear perception in Molière's audience of a norm of fashionable dress. The 1682 engravings update modish attire in the amoureux, as a comparison of the 1662 and 1682 engravings of L'Ecole des maris will show (nos. 5 and 6, respectively); it was obviously essential to depict the lover in full conformity with fashions as they evolved. From a norm of dress, we may also infer standards of conduct, especially in the rites of courtship; it is no accident that suitors are shown not only in elegant, upper-class dress but often in a position of courtly deference to the beloved. Effects of contrast underline yet more this perceived hegemony of taste. The lover's elegance is emphasized by the eccentric attire worn by the clownish Sganarelle in *L'Ecole des maris* (no. 6) and by the same character in *Le Mariage forcé* (no. 11). A similar juxtaposition highlights number sixteen as well. Harpagon's antiquated *bourgeois* dress (no. 18) enhances Valère's modish costume, more that of the lover than the house manager (he is the *intendant* of Harpagon's household), all the more since there is a second contrast with Maître Jacques's slovenly cook's garb. We may infer then from Brissart's illustrations and those of Chauveau before him that the audience attributed great importance to the romantic or courtship element in Molière's theater, and more generally that a highly visible presence in comedy of an upper-class elite was central to the spectator's pleasure. That these costumes were associated at close range with the attire worn by the young blades who made it a habit to sit on the stage could only reinforce the sense of exemplarity.

The young gallant does not betray in his behavior the expectations placed upon him by his dress. The meetings, for example, of Cléante, Elise, and Mariane in *L'Avare* (3.6) display the courtesy and formality of children to the manner born. That Cléante and Elise could be the offspring of a dehumanized acquisitor evidently created no sense of *invraisemblance* among the spectators; they were accustomed to hear the Pantalone of the *comédiens italiens* speak in a Venetian dialect whereas his daughter's discourse was in the finest Italian; similarly a priapic *vecchio* could have offspring with the best manners. The imperatives of entertainment prevailed over any psychological sense of realism; and true to this tradition, Molière showed to the end, with *Le Malade imaginaire,* a clownish, doting simpleton who had fathered a sensitive, cultivated, and proper young lady. Angélique, with Cléante, so at ease with "le bel air des choses," constitutes, like other lovers, a kind of truewit center to the play and only underlines further Argan's fatuity, the ludicrous antics of the medical team, and Béline's venality.

Even when the antisocial forces tend to dominate the whole play—*L'Ecole des femmes* and *Tartuffe,* for example—notions of exemplariness, though not advocated by articulate characters, can be inferred from the text itself. Thus when Arnolphe fulminates against "ruelles," "femmes d'esprit," "femmes habiles," he questions the whole of polite society, organized as it was around witty, socially adept ladies of rank and merit. As he plays the role of a conceited, wrongheaded fool, he validates by implication the values of this salon world. Similarly, in *Tartuffe,* we do not behold Elmire's social circle and can only infer the tone that must have dominated it from the self-possessed, resourceful, and well-mannered woman whom we do observe. As well, Tartuffe's hypocritical fulminations serve only to confirm this impression. In addition, Horace in the first play and Damis, Valère, and Mariane in the second, convey by appearance and conduct, however much they are overshadowed, the social propriety that Moliére generally gives to the *amoureux,* and the magnanimity they show when put to the test; Damis's reconciliation with his deceived father and Valére's well-meaning if futile plan to spirit Orgon away from Tartuffe's vengeful machinations.

In other plays, however, *le bel air des choses* moves from the wings or from a somewhat subordinate position to a more central role. Here the lovers are more worldly wise, the rites of *galanterie* more explicitly delineated, and the overall tone more sophisticated, more bantering. In short, the plays now to be studied approximate most closely in Molière the tone of Restoration manners comedy. Significantly, Brissart depicts a gallant/young lady pair in many of them.

A good illustration may be found in *La Comtesse d'Escarbagnas.* Although set in the provinces, this one-act play offers two perspectives on Paris. The ridiculous country countess exudes a confused, undiscriminating infatuation with the capital based upon a whirlwind visit. On the other hand, Julie and the Vicomte have the intrinsic qualities that make them proper representatives of Parisian sophistication. Since the Vicomte is expected to purvey all the latest court gossip (scene 1), we may assume that he is a part-time habitué of high social circles in the capital. The truewit role of this couple is twofold: they interpret for us, as our accomplices, the foolishness and pretention they see around them; we relish their mocking comments behind the Comtesse's back and their thinly disguised irony in statements directly to her. They convey as well positive images of *le bel air*. As longtime initiates in the mysteries of courtship, they play the game of *galanterie* with distinction and finesse. A respectful, obedient lover, the Vicomte carries on mock wooing of the Comtesse at Julie's behest. He presents Julie with a sonnet in the best *précieux* style, the only poetic homage by an exemplary character in all of Molière. It is no coincidence that in the Brissart engraving (no. 22), Julie and the Vicomte may be seen on either side of the Comtesse, an elegant frame for the ridiculous lady listening to her son's Latin lessons recited before the pedantic magister Bobinet, dressed in professorial black.

Molière's first comédie-ballet, *Les Fâcheux*, conveys social distinction in yet another way. The décor represents a public space, but unlike the conventional "maisons et rues" setting of *L'Ecole des femmes,* this thoroughfare, an "allée" in a fashionable but unnamed garden, caters to the well-bred who come and go, along with the *fâcheux,* on their ritual social rounds. It is there that Eraste seeks out his lady, Orphise, in competition with other gallants. This rhythm of casual encounters in various fashionable places is, we recall, a hallmark of Restoration comedy; and the improvisational character of *Les Fâcheux,* the impression of freedom and spontaneity in human happenings, confirms the resemblance. Eraste's standing as a truewit needs no further proof than his costume, the colorful, elegant dress of the fashionable courtier set off by the customary wig (no. 7). The whole is emphasized by his valet's plebeian dress. A man of obvious means, he is able, we learn from an earlier speech, to pay the high price of a seat on the stage; his attentiveness and discretion as a spectator form a laudable backdrop for the noisy, inopportune arrival of another member of the audience. The latter also takes his place on the stage but in the center, not on the sides where the stage seats were normally placed. As a result he impedes the view of most of the groundlings. Eraste's irritation at the accumulated breaches of social norms that cascade upon him further confirm his role as an arbiter of taste and propriety. Although the courtship scenes are sketchy, our gentleman is obviously a sophisticated *galant* too, at ease in the rituals of wooing.

Though set in a private salon, *La Critique de l'Ecole des femmes* more closely approximates the tone of good-humored, freewheeling conversation that so often imbues Restoration comedy. It is also a play strongly polarized between true and false wit. Just as people of taste are set off against fops and fools in English manners comedy, so are the truewits of *La Critique*—Elise, Uranie, and Dorante (a *chevalier* and therefore a member of the lower nobility)—depicted in sharp opposition to affected prudes like Climène, hare-brained fops like the *marquis,* or humorless bookmen like Lysidas. Again, costume provides unmistakable indicators as to appropriate audience reaction. On the right of the 1682 engraving (no. 9), we distinguish a well-dressed gentleman seated between two elegant ladies—undoubtedly our three truewits—and as an antithetical block, we behold Lysidas in his dull, bourgeois costume, the *marquis* next to him in flamboyant contrast, and, in the middle, Climène, her neck and shoulders chastely covered with a *fichu* of some kind.

The conversation, though occasionally heated, never degenerates into acrimony. Even the fools stop short of total unseemliness, and the truewits are always at pains to lighten the atmosphere when necessary. Thus Elise resorts opportunely to irony when Dorante becomes a shade too impassioned: "J'ai changé d'avis," she declares, and ostensibly goes over to Climène's side of the argument. Dorante, true to his gallant and decorous nature, immediately picks up the cue: "Je me dédirai pour l'amour de vous, de tout ce que j'ai dit" (scene 5). Again, at the end when the *marquis's* raucous braying brings the conversation to a halt, a mood of detached good humor suddenly sets in. The conversation becomes a play, the free-wheeling *dispute* turns into a projected theatrical text. Real people are suddenly roles: "Je fournirais de bon coeur mon personnage," says Elise; and the dialogue takes on a genre shape when it ends appropriately with a banquet.

For English commentators, Molière's distinctive manners comedy is *Le Misanthrope*. Its upper-class, "genteel" setting and its scintillating display of wit give it indeed a special place in the Molière canon. More significantly, however, it deals more than any other comedy with questions of social procedure as distinct from moral considerations. In fact, it demonstrates that society will not tolerate absolutes like uncompromising sincerity and offers the same pessimistic explanation as that of the Restoration: man's vanity and selfishness blind him to the truth. Here La Rochefoucauld and Pascal speak with the same voice: if society cannot stand plain-speaking, then it is condemned to live on appearances, "mines," for each must disguise himself to his neighbor. So comedy, along with defending by implication the nature of civilized society, assumes the satirical task of exposing falsity and stripping mankind of hollow pretenses. This acerbic mission reaches its apogee in the bitterest of Restoration playwrights, Wycherley; it is no surprise that he chose *Le Misanthrope* as the starting point for *The Plain-Dealer.* Yet too much is usually made of obvious surface resemblances. Like *Le Misanthrope* it is a curiously ambivalent play, but its satire is much more general and more biting. On the other hand, its ending is discordantly romantic. Manly, far from going into a self-imposed solitary exile, will apparently wed Fidelia (the approximate counterpart of Eliante), who, disguised as a young seaman, has waited doggedly for Manly to appreciate his/her devotion.

It is customary to categorize two characters in Molière's play as exemplary, or truewit, types: Philinte and Eliante. The former's tact, sensitivity, and tolerance make him an eminently social being; his dress underscores the rightness of this attribution, if we take as evidence the splendid costume of the gallant depicted in the 1682 engraving (no. 14) and in the ealier anonymous 1667 depiction (no. 13). Unlike the Restoration hero, however, he lacks an important attribute: wit. He may possess it in the general sense of social decorum, but what he says is curiously flat; in his tendency to pontificate, he keeps a distance from the jollity he sees around him. Despite her more episodic role, Eliante carries more value as social entertainment. Her lighthearted speech on the illusions with which men in love clothe their ladies (vv. 711–30) is a true exercise in verbal wit, sustained, clever, decorous. However, the real burden of wit, so to speak, is assumed by Célimène. If *le bel air* consists in sharp repartee, entertaining disputatiousness, sophisticated charm, she embodies these qualities more than any other character in the play and perhaps in all of Molière. Her teasing, confident way of handling Alceste reminds us of such self-possessed Restoration gentlewomen as Millamant. In the salon scene (2.4), clever character sketches and lapidary quips come tumbling out as her irrepressible inclination to wit, seconded by her admirers, urges her on. Her devastating comparison of Cléon, for instance, to an insipid dish of food owes its impact to word play around the verb *servir* (vv. 623–30). She handles Arsinoé (3.4) with a cutting deftness that shows her command of language: her long retort is a spontaneous yet sustained parody of what she has just heard. She picks up each phrase in Arsinoé's set piece and drives her point home with a verbatim repetition of the concluding three lines of Arsinoé's accusatory speech (vv. 958–60; 910–12). In short, Célimène has a mastery of utterance that puts her on par with the best of Restoration gentlewomen. It may be countered that she is given to backbiting and double-dealing, a propensity that brings her to temporary ruin. These criticisms betray, however, a narrowly moral view of *esprit*. Restoration comedy does not confine wit to generous, if clever, comments about others; truewits mock the embodiments of false wits often to their faces, under cover of irony, and certainly behind their back as part of the social game.

If Célimène is analogous to the Restoration gentlewoman—

refined, emancipated, self-indulgent, reveling in the homage paid to her by a claque of admirers, basically virtuous despite Arsinoé's innuendoes—what is lacking in this play, what keeps it at a distance from Restoration comedy, is the other half of the spirited couple. Rather than place a Mirabell opposite his sharp-witted lady, Molière chose to couple her to a boor. Alceste's wilfully antisocial pose, his self-defeating moral absolutes put him at the farthest remove from the gentleman of English comedy. In consequence the whole mood of the play darkens as we near the curtain time. Alceste's raging proviso scene with its demand that Célimène join him in "mon désert où j'ai fait voeu de vivre" (v. 1763) contrasts in every respect with the lighthearted conjugal negotiations between Mirabell and Millamant at the end of *The Way of the World.*

The cynicism of Restoration comedy has always troubled those who wish to equate social procedure with moral imperatives. That a rake like Horner in *The Country Wife,* lustful seducer of the inexperienced, gleeful maker of cuckolds, shameless deceiver, articulate debunker of all conventional wisdom—that such a character could be a truewit (as Fujimura in fact defines him [p. 239]) may appear to justify such skepticism. In this light, Célimène's *médisance* and hypocrisy are mere peccadillos. But in two other plays, Molière portrays the gallant in pursuits that, by the canons of strict morality, are dishonorable. In one, *George Dandin,* the suitor forms part of the classic triangle involving a complaisant wife and a foolish husband; the second, *Le Bourgeois gentilhomme,* features a high-ranking nobleman, Dorante, who shamelessly bilks Monsieur Jourdain of vast sums in order to finance his own lavish courtship of Dorimène. Can a cuckolder and a *chevalier d'industrie* be properly placed in the truewit category?

Molière had already anticipated the cuckold triangle in a short comédie-ballet, *Le Mariage forcé.* Italianate in inspiration, it features largely a succession of Latin-spouting pedants in the line of the *dottori.* The slender plot carries no direct allusion to Paris mores, but the kind of life enjoyed by Célimène in *Le Misanthrope* is

a key aspiration of the young lady Dorimène whom the fool Sganarelle is finally forced to marry. Similarly coquettish in temperament (*galante* is the word attributed to her [scene 1]), she hates
solitude and prefers "le jeu, les visites, les assemblées, les cadeaux
et les promenades, en un mot, toutes les choses de plaisir" (scene
2). These hedonistic expectations are perfectly consistent with the
easy *art de vivre* of the capital, as is the ideal of an aristocratic marriage based on trust where husband and wife can live "comme
deux personnes qui savent leur monde" (ibid.). There is indeed a
hint of upper-class rank: Dorimène appears with a distinctive status symbol, a train carried by a boy (scene 2), and the 1682 engraving depicting the scene where her brother challenges Sganarelle to
a duel (a provocation reserved for people of rank) shows a young
man dressed as a person of quality (no. 11). Dorimène is courted by
a gallant named Lycaste, and their exchanges, though brief, carry
the tone of decorous courtship. When one adds Sganarelle's contrasting view of marriage—a means of creating innumerable
clones of himself and possessing the duly itemized components of
Dorimène's appetizing anatomy (scene 1)—we can well speak of a
truewit perspective in this play despite its skimpy manners
content.

Yet all this presumed exemplariness is devalued by context. A
tone of cynicism makes Dorimène's profession of freedom actually
a recipe for license. She rushes off to buy suitable clothing and
expects Sganarelle to settle with the merchants (scene 2), conduct
that anticipates her blithe answer to Lycaste, angered at her apparent betrayal: "Je vous considère toujours de même, et ce mariage ne doit point vous inquiéter: c'est un homme que je n'épouse
point par amour, et sa seule richesse me fait résoudre à l'accepter"
(scene 7). Lycaste is probably more inclined to have Dorimène as
his mistress than as a wife, and in words heavy with insolence he
tells Sganarelle: "Je veux faire amitié avec vous, et lier ensemble
un petit commerce de visites et divertissements" (ibid.). This is the
cynical tone of Restoration comedy, where comic butts deserve
their fate and marital obligations are treated with the greatest

casualness. Such is the way of the world, and the truewit perspective here stresses justified self-indulgence over a conventional morality that protects the fool.

The plot of *George Dandin* is built upon the same triangle. Indeed, *Le Mariage forcé* can be thought of as a prologue to this better-known satire of the *paysan-gentilhomme*. There are some permutations, of course; the marriage has been forced upon the wife, not the husband, and our sympathies tend to be with the victim this time. Angélique's view of marriage is identical with that enunciated by Dorimène: refusal of solitude, defense of social life: "Je trouve bons [les maris] de vouloir qu'on soit morte à tous les divertissements, et qu'on ne vive que pour eux. Je me moque de cela, et ne veux point mourir si jeune" (2.2). Again, Dandin's image of a conjugal "chaîne" (ibid.) stands in devalued opposition to an aristocratic norm. Like Dorimène, Angélique has a gallant. Here the Paris perspective is explicit: we learn early on that Clitandre is a "jeune courtisan" who carries into the provinces the best manners of the capital: "Que dans tous leurs discours et dans toutes leurs actions les gens de cour ont un air agréable!" (2.3), marvels Angélique. This time the gallant is given named rank, that of *vicomte*, and an active courtship role. Clitandre's well-spoken and urbane conduct forms an effective contrast with Dandin's crudeness. In short, rather than being moral reprobates, as some critics would have them,[7] Angélique and Clitandre approximate a truewit couple representing the aristocratic manners of "la Ville" so strongly opposed to Dandin's rough ways. And in such a world, the witless pay the bill with no indulgence from other characters or from us.

Le Bourgeois gentilhomme presents a different problem. A traditional pair of young lovers already carries a romantic love interest, and some stress is laid on their exemplariness. We have seen how Cléonte defines his social status with honesty and precision, refusing to inflate his rank to that of *gentilhomme*. But we also behold a seasoned, mature couple reminiscent of Julie and the Vicomte in that other satire of social pretention, *La Comtesse d'Escarbagnas*. Dorante is a man of the world who recognizes good breeding: he praises Cléonte as "un fort galant homme et qui mérite que l'on s'intéresse pour lui" (5. 2). He is a man of wit, as is evidenced by his sparkling gastronomical speech (however recondite the modern reader may find it) (4.1). His courtship of the young widow, Dorimène, passes through all the proper ritual steps as recapitulated by his lady: "Les visites fréquentes ont commencé; les déclarations sont venues ensuite, qui après elles ont traîné les sérénades et les cadeaux que les présents ont suivis" (3. 15). This is the *galanterie* to which both the Dorimène of *Le Mariage forcé* and the Angélique of *George Dandin* ardently aspire.

To be sure, Jourdain subsidizes this courtship to which he offers such a gross caricature. Dorante's willingness to use the burgher's money for his own ends, together with his insolence toward Madame Jourdain, has led critics to label him a *chevalier d'industrie,* an unscrupulous adventurer.[8] Lest the burgher's wife gain too much by the comparison, however, it must be remembered that Madame Jourdain is discourteous to Dorante and almost everyone else; her temperament is so carping and humorless that we can scarcely identify with it, whatever approval we may give the precepts she utters. Molière's intentions are all the more evident in that he assigned the character to a male actor, Hubert. Dorante, on the other hand, has a strongly positive role as purveyor of entertainment, defender of young love, and finally future husband. A true "knight of the industry" may be found in Etherege's *She Would if She Could,* where Mr. Rake-hell more than lives up to his name. The newly rich merchant eager for status was fair game for everyone from the king down. No opprobrium could have been directed against a gentleman like Dorante, who offered value for money, consideration for cash, especially if his own status was validated by noble rank and by a demonstrable gentility of behavior.

No analysis of social norms in Molière would be complete without some discussion of auxiliaries. Comparisons with Restoration comedy will prove less fruitful, however, because there the servant class carried less dramatic and comic value than in Molière. Sometimes auxiliaries recede so far into the background that they are anonymous: "valet," "footman," and so on. On the other hand, they may enjoy brief cameo roles, such as Dorimant's servant Jeremy in *Love for Love,* a winning bumbler and pretender to wit; or Mincing, the affected *suivante* to Millamant in *The Way of the World*; in addition, "Mademoiselle," Lady Fancifull's woman in *The Provok'd Wife,* makes a fitting pair with her mistress in her French-inspired airs. But such individualized types are rare. On the whole, servants are two-dimensional identities with episodic roles; appearing infrequently and briefly, they leave center stage to their superiors in rank.

The importance of comparable characters in Molière needs no emphasizing. Not only do they carry great comic force but they are integrated into the very structure of the play by their typical support of the love interest. Molière, as a disciple of the *commedia dell'arte,* held to a tradition of reliance upon auxiliaries so strong that servant types were spawned or kept alive long after the final decay of the genre: Pierrot and Harlequin come immediately to mind. The servant polarized into two subtypes: The first *zanni* tended to be a resourceful, exuberant fellow to whom Molière gave his own enduring stamp in Scapin; a second, bumbling valet gave a different kind of comic effect—that produced by the doltish Alain and Georgette of *L'Ecole des femmes* or Du Bois in *Le Misanthrope,* whose thick-headedness so enrages his master Alceste. But in general, Molière found the avatar of the tricky slave more useful to his comic purposes and adds to the traditional inventiveness a marked streak of insolence. Here we find such memorable *soubrettes* as Dorine in *Tartuffe,* Nicole in *Le Bourgeois gentilhomme,* Toinette in *Le Malade imaginaire,* or a manservant like La Flèche in *L'Avare,* whose theft of the *cassette* brings the plot to a climax.

In all these instances, servants side with young love against the master of the house. They thus add substance to the truewit core of the play, for by supporting the courteous young gallants and the ladies of their choice, they help sponsor the norms that the couple is meant to embody. Through Nicole and Covielle, for instance, Molière may poke fun at the rhetoric of *galanterie;* but by associating their marriage with that of Julie and Cléonte, and of Dorante and Dorimène, the author places them in the same institutional value structure. It is especially noteworthy that well-founded, if insolent, protestations by servants are often paired with admonitions offered by more serious characters. In *Tartuffe,* Dorine's colorful language embroiders comically upon Clèante's heavy-handed strictures; the Toinette of *Le Malade imaginaire* is in league with the eloquent, well-spoken Béralde but makes her point by daring facetiousness. La Flèche's scathing assessment of Harpagon's character (*L'Avare*) forms a comic counterpoint to the bitter expostulations by the miser's son, Cléante. Indeed, one senses that Molière used such impertinence to lighten the comic mood and in order to counterbalance disputatious dialogue. There is no such character in *Les Femmes savantes,* for instance, for the commonsense views of a Martine are not sustained beyond a scene or two—whence the especially argumentative tone compared, say, to another well-wrought five-act play in verse like *Tartuffe.*

Such characters are so vividly drawn, their opinions seem so right and their courage so admirable, that they often are taken as proofs of Molière's supposed affection for *le bon peuple.* Such may have been his feelings as a person, but his comic presentations of the lower classes betray the biases inherent in the social outlook of his audience and its presiding apex, "la Cour et la Ville." Dorine's lapses of taste are explained away by her humble status: Molière feels constrained to tell us in a stage direction that "c'est une servante qui parle" (*Tartuffe,* v. 195). A similar attitude of condescension envelops the lower strata of society from the peasants and fisherfolk of *Dom Juan* to the stolid mercantilism espoused by Madame Jourdain. Servants may complain, but they are made to offer no searching criticism of society; their ideology is that of their masters. Although incapable by low birth of ever assuming *les belles manières* or even understanding the intricacies of upper-class behavior, their loyalty to the social hierarchy and their grudging acceptance of their place in it implies an adherence to the norms that Molière's comedy celebrates. Witless by nature, auxiliaries are truewits out of solidarity.

Chapter 4

"Apes and Echoes": Provincial Pretenders and Capital Lackwits

In contrast to the truewits, the coterie of privileged insiders, the rest of the world consists chiefly of a formless mass of humanity carrying a mark of exclusion by reason of faulty judgment, poor breeding, or basic incompatibility. Two chapters will now be devoted to the subgroups of otherness, those representing some particular species of false wit.

Provincial Pretenders

A first level of estrangement is geographical: the true appreciation of the scintillating life of the capital is denied all those who live beyond it. This observation holds, of course, for those who live outside the confines of the nation, but xenophobic stereotypes are not typical of Molière's comedies or of those from the Restoration manners tradition. Although a general Gallomania pervaded English mores, especially in Charles II's reign, English comedies show, admittedly, a certain ambivalence toward France: affectation, as with Sir Fopling Flutter, the Gallicized fop of *The Man of Mode,* can be taken as a benign French disease, in contrast with the more serious Gallic malady responsible for Horner's alleged impotence in *The Country Wife.* An allusion in the latter play to the licentious novel *L'Ecole des filles* suggests that France was also a ready source of libertine material. But in general, Restoration comedy depicts homegrown manners, and even the blockheads are thoroughly English.

Molière's portrayal of the non-French world centers on the Mediterranean. A number of his plays are set in the conventional Italy of the *commedia dell'arte,* but this locale suggests no xenophobic satire but rather a sunny, exuberant, romantic world. The true alien in Molière's theater is the Moor; outside of one disparaging allusion to the moneylending Jew (*L'Avare,* 2. 1), itself coupled with the word "arabe," Molière confines his jibes to a stereotyped image of Muslim manners, especially as regards man/woman relationships. In opposition to the French ideal of the *galant homme,* the Arab is scorned as a pathologically jealous, passionately vindictive watchdog warily guarding a harem of humiliated and servile females. Molière built a short play, *Le Sicilien,* largely on this antithesis. True, Don Pèdre is nominally a European, but he has the soul of a Muslim; as he himself declares to his mistress, "Je suis jaloux comme un tigre, et, si vous voulez, comme un diable. Mon amour vous veut toute à moi" (scene 6). In contrast Adraste, "gentilhomme français," embodies the chief attributes of his fellow countrymen. As his lady, Isidore, comments admiringly, "Les Français ont quelque chose en eux de poli, de galant, que n'ont pas les autres nations" (scene 13). This comparison of Arab-like possessiveness, jealousy, and sequestration with French high-mindedness and aristocratic liberalism had already been suggested in *L'Ecole des femmes,* where Arnolphe's view of man's domination of woman coincides with Muslim stereotypes even to the "lord and master" harem formula (v. 712). Similarly, the soubrette of *L'Ecole des maris,* Lisette, stands up impudently against Sganarelle's tyrannical behavior by comparing it to the aberrations of the infidel: "Sommes-nous chez les Turcs à renfermer les gens?" (v. 144).

These xenophobic touches are rare, however. The most significant geographical antithesis to the capital relates to the outback of one's own nation. Muir's remark that Restoration comedy "presents a contrast between metropolitan and provincial manners" (p. 11) applies equally to Molière. Life in the provinces, in both France and England, is unfailingly depicted as gross and tedious, and those country folk who seek a way of refinement in the capital can eke out but a caricature of high society.

Among countless examples in Restoration comedy, one may cite Mrs. Sullen's explosion of rage against "country pleasures": "Dost think, child, that my limbs were made for leaping of ditches and clambering over stiles; or that my parents wisely foreseeing my future happiness in country pleasures had early instructed me in the rural accomplishments of drinking fat ale, playing at whiste and smoking tobacco with my husband?" (Farquhar, *The Beaux' Strategem*, 2. 1). In a more lighthearted vein, at the conclusion of *The Man of Mode* Harriet warns her betrothed, Dorimant, of the country life that awaits them in "a great, rambling, lone house. . . . There you'll find my mother, an old lame aunt, and myself, sir, perched up on chairs at a distance in a large parlour, sitting moping like three or four melancholy birds in a spacious volary. . . . Methinks I hear the hateful cry of rooks already—kaw, kaw, kaw. There's music to the worst cry in London. . . ." (5. 2).

A comparable disdain for small-town life and rural amusements permeates Dorine's warning to Mariane should the young lady become Tartuffe's spouse:

Vous irez par le coche en sa petite ville,
Qu'en oncles et cousins vous trouverez fertile,
Et vous vous plairez fort à les entretenir.
D'abord chez le beau monde on vous fera venir;
Vour irez visiter, pour votre bienvenue,
Madame la baillive et Madame l'élue
Qui d'un siège pliant vous feront honorer

[vv. 657-663]

Trivial pastimes, a stultifying social life with the graceless wives of minor local officials—such is the destiny proposed to a young, comely, and well-bred Parisian lady. The rural accomplishments detailed by Mrs. Sullen bring us closer to the farmhouse and the ultimate indignity of perpetual confinement with one's husband, but the satirical thrust is the same. The matter can be summarized by two pithy sayings, one from an English country knight, "A man had better be a vagabond in this town [London] than a justice of the peace in the country" (*She Would if She Could,* 1.1), and the familiar quip by the valet-fop Mascarille in *Les Précieuses ridicules,* "Hors de Paris il n'y a point de salut pour les honnêtes gens" (scene 9).

Since English manners comedy takes place almost exclusively in London itself, provincials are necessarily depicted as intruders. The most significant exception, *The Beaux' Stratagem,* set in Lichfield, nonetheless presents provincial life from a London standpoint, as is evident from the passage just quoted. Mrs. Sullen's husband is labeled, moreover, "a country blockhead," and another character, Lady Bountifull, an "old civil country gentlewoman," is but a female country knight.

Restoration countryfolk may embody rough ways without aping Town polish, but Molière invariably portrays provincials not only as gross bumpkins (or their female equivalents) but as ludicrous pretenders. Like the *hobereaux* in *George Dandin,* they may make what are seen as fraudulent demands for respect or they may actually aspire to a higher social station or to a level of elegance comparable to that of Paris. Or, worst of all, they may try to elbow their way directly into the capital, always with humiliating results.

In *George Dandin,* as a matter of fact, we find the harshest portrait of provincial life that Molière ever conveyed. The country nobility as personified by Monsieur et Madame de Sotenville are treated with the same contempt as that reserved for the English country knight. Their quaint ways denote a ludicrous reverence for the past, whereas manners comedy always celebrates the best in the here and now. Costume is a further telling indicator of such attitudes, and the attire worn by the characters in *George Dandin* is no exception. In the Brissart engraving of 1682 (no. 17), Sotenville sports an antiquated costume grotesquely reminiscent of knighthood days; Madame de Sotenville, true to her Prudoterie descendence, spreads a high shawl around the entire upper part of her body, and a kerchief hides almost all her hair. Opposite her we notice an attractive young lady, Angélique, Dandin's wife, fashionably dressed with the usual low neckline and a *fichu* set back far enough on the head to reveal her becoming tresses. Were Clitandre portrayed too, we would no doubt see an avatar of the many young gallants depicted in the 1682 engravings. With Sotenville the fierce pride of the feudal baron undergoes a demeaning caricature consonant with absolutist ideology. Speaking of his daughter's possible adultery, he exclaims: "Corbleu! je lui passerais mon épée au travers du corps, à elle et au galant, si elle avait forfait à son honneur" (1. 4). Along with futile hyperbole go empty forms. His lessons in nobility center on making his son-in-law address him and his family properly. Dandin himself underscores the tawdriness of provincial life with his native boorishness matched by an ambition for rank that turns him into Monsieur de la Dandinière. Like Sir John Brute, he is ill-mannered and hostile to his spouse: "I dare not draw my sword, tho' even to get rid of my Wife," laments the knight; "Il me prend des tentations d'accommoder tout son visage à la compote" (2. 2), as Dandin confides in an aside. This mixture of vulgarity and pretentiousness is made concrete in his dress (no. 17): his high heels suggest noble rank, but he wears a frockcoat, not the *justaucorps* sported by the upper-class gallants, and no periwig graces his head.

In *La Comtesse d'Escarbagnas,* Molière depicts not only the trivial and dull world of the provincial *hobereaux* but also a ridiculous attempt to impose upon that world the outward forms of Paris urbanity. The Comtesse's salon actualizes the image of endless petty social rituals conveyed by Dorine in *Tartuffe.* In her effort to emulate Paris life after a brief visit to the capital, the Comtesse assembles a motley collection of small-town dignitaries, all tainted with professionalism: Monsieur Tibaudier, a man of law; the tax collector, Monsieur Harpin; and the young Count's *précepteur,* Monsieur Bobinet, a rank pedant whose Latinizing lessons displease even the Comtesse herself. The truewit elegance of the sophisticated couple Julie and the Vicomte is emphasized by the inept wooing by the Comtesse's admirers, and the Vicomte's clever sonnet finds its ironic counterpart in the contrived examples of false wit with which the play abounds. Thus the ponderous pear imagery of Monsieur Tibaudier's complaint to his *belle dame sans merci*: "Les poires ne sont pas encore bien mûres, mais elles en cadrent mieux avec la dureté de votre âme, qui, par ses continuels dédains, ne me promet pas poires molles" (scene 4). He himself does not speak this *billet doux*; it is delivered to the Comtesse and read obligingly by the Vicomte, who takes advantage of the occasion, no doubt, to lay a heavy weight of sarcasm on the labored lamentation. Later Tibaudier declaims further tasteless homage to his lady, amid ironic laments by his mock rival, the Vicomte, such as "Je suis perdu après cela" . . . "Me voilà supplanté, moi, par Monsieur Tibaudier" (scene 5).

A more comically effective image of countryfolk is to be found in the plays set in the capital. By showing provincials in direct contact with Paris gentlefolk, Molière makes the most of their comic value. Restoration playwrights resorted characteristically to the same stereotypes that go back at least as far as Jonson's country gulls and Shakespeare's presentation of bumbling if loveable rustics. The tags attached to the dramatis personae reinforce familiar prejudices. In *Love for Love,* Congreve describes Miss Prue as "a silly awkward country girl"; Sullen, a character in *The Beaux' Strategem,* is "a country blockhead, brutal to his wife." A more endearing provincial, Sir Wilfull Witwoud, is depicted in *The Way of the World.* Fresh from his village, he cannot understand the polished mores of the Town. Astounded at the idleness of London late-risers for whom morning lasts a good part of the day, he remarks: "We should count it toward afternoon in our parts, down in Shropshire" (3. 3). Rough and ready in affection, he is offended at the formality shown to him by his half-brother, a would-be sophisticate: "tis not modish," the latter points out, "to know relations in town. You think you're in the country, where great lubbery brothers slabber and kiss one another when they

meet . . . tis not the fashion here" (3.3). This witless perspective on Town life carries here a gentle irony regarding fashion and anticipates such amiable rustics as Bob Acres in Sheridan's *The Rivals.*
A forcefully contrasting image obtains in the most celebrated country personage in all of Restoration comedy, Margery Pinchwife, the heroine of *The Country Wife.* The very title invites comparison, of course, with a "town wife," cultivated enough to be a social asset but sufficiently astute as well to wreak vengeance on a churlish husband. Here Wycherley has elaborated upon a key thematic antithesis found in *L'Ecole des femmes,* his main source of literary inspiration. Molière develops systematically a comparison between the "femme d'esprit" and the "idiote," the "femme habile" and the "sotte." Wycherley underlines the geographical implications of the contrast: "I have married no London wife," declares Margery's defiant husband; "she has no beauty but her youth, no attraction but her modesty, wholesome, homely and huswifely; that's all" (1. 1). Agnès was reared as well at a great distance from sophisticated circles, in a country convent; but the romantic premises of Molière's plot confer innate gentility upon her. Wellborn already through her father, Enrique, she has but to blossom under the right circumstances. Margery, on the other hand, is a true small-town girl who must learn London ways from experience, "be taught breeding," to borrow Horner's caustic pun. Yet, lacking the essential discrimination and judgment, she will never assimilate the natural inborn grace and polish of a Town gentlewoman like Mrs. Millamant. Horner's aphorism is especially apt, given Molière's implied praise of the "femme d'esprit" (v. 105): "Wit is more necessary than beauty; and I think no young woman ugly that has it, and no handsome woman agreeable without it" (1. 1). Lacking the protection of proper upbringing against a nascent sensuality, Margery becomes easy prey. It is only with the utmost difficulty that she becomes dimly aware of the genteel Town virtue of discretion. Horner's well-advertised fiction of impotence has gained him access to all the boudoirs of London. After

a dangerous moment of near exposure, Horner keeps his cover at play's end and his rake's progress bids fair to continue for some distance. Margery, like Lady Fidget, has received convincing proof of Horner's manhood, but unlike her practiced partner in adultery, Margery wishes to proclaim the truth: "You shall not disparage poor Mr. Horner, for to my certain knowledge . . ." (5.4) and her mouth is quickly stopped up. Finally, with some reluctance she agrees to "tell more lies" (i.e., to bow to the way of the world) and preserve thereby her own pleasures.

This vivid portrait of a country wife should not make us forget that Pinchwife himself is a kind of country husband. The text suggests that he has spent a long period of time in the provinces and has so lost contact with prevailing Town fashions that Horner mocks "the slovenliness of [his] habit" (1. 1). His manner of expression carries the callousness of the backwoods boor: the dowry he is about to bestow on behalf of his sister to Sparkish, his future brother-in-law, becomes meretricious mercantilism: "I must give him five thousand pounds to lie with my sister" (1. 1). His jealousy surpasses in its ferocity even Arnolphe's passionate possessiveness. Although fear of cuckoldry is, as we shall see later, a fault ascribed routinely to the "citizen" in London and the Paris merchant class, Pinchwife speaks here for a backward and repressive kind of life that manners comedy associates with the country.

These examples suffice to illustrate the London snobbery that stigmatized life beyond the capital and heaped ridicule upon provincial intruders. Molière catered to the same kind of scorn not only in his direct portrayal of country life but also in those comedies where the provincial tries to make his way in Paris. We shall see that Molière adds to the innate grossness of such characters the self-ignorance that makes them social climbers as well. We come then to the provincial witwoud and his or her effort to win status in the brilliant center of the nation.

The presumed intent of the playwright's first resounding success, *Les Précieuses ridicules*, remains a problem even today. Construed in the past as a broadside against the reigning salon ladies of the day, defended by Molière himself as a satire of affectation, the comedy betrays a certain ambivalence toward that elusive social phenomenon called *préciosité*. Without trying to unravel the intricacies of the question, we may say that the impulse which gives rise to the *précieux* movement seems analogous to that which gives life in England to the notion of wit. The distaste for the vulgar or the banal, the cultivation of new, clever, decorous modes of expression consonant with a distinguished style of life and its external signs (dress, cultural icons, circles of frequentation, etc.)—all this fits the general code of an upper-class coterie. Inasmuch as Molière catered to such elitist pretentions, he has rightly been called a *précieux* himself.[1] Yet La Grange in *Les Précieuses* puts a clearly derogatory stamp on the word when he laments that "l'air précieux n'a pas seulement infecté Paris, il s'est aussi répandu dans les provinces" (scene 1). This image of toxicity coming from what seems to be a truewit character has given pause to many a critic. Yet we observed earlier that the line between true and false wit could be very tenuous, since wit is contrived by its very nature. Just as *esprit* merges often into affected wit, so *préciosité* as a legitimate striving for distinction can betray a ludicrous underside of labored effort and narrow snobbishness. This danger is inherent in any group that defines itself as the happy few, for it must develop a set of rules, a mode of expression that will affirm and justify its aloofness. The *précieux* seem to have narrowed the elite circle beyond that which had already been established by "la Cour et la Ville," thereby sponsoring unduly restrictive norms and challenging those in place. We may then take Molière's protestations at face value: he is condemning false wit, not the thrust behind wit in general.

And are La Grange and Du Croisy truewits after all? Among all the young suitors in Molière's theater, they are the only ones ostensibly wearing ordinary clothing. They are not portrayed in the 1682 engravings, but the Précieuses complain of their dull mode of dress: "venir en visite amoureuse avec une jambe toute unie, un chapeau désarmé de plumes, une tête irrégulière en cheveux, un habit qui souffre une indigence de rubans . . ." (scene 4). This is clearly not the splendid attire worn by the typical gallant. With their plain hats, their undecorated costumes, and especially their wigless heads, they are far from the image of the blue-blooded suitor. Admittedly the Précieuses' notion of fashionable dress is that displayed later by the flamboyant Mascarille, but it seems plausible that the actual costume worn by La Grange and Du Croisy represents the other extreme, that of middle-class sobriety. It is noteworthy, moreover, that they have come not to court their ladies but to become acquainted with their future spouses. Although a proper young blade would not go to the absurd extremes of the *galanterie* demanded by the Précieuses, La Grange and Du Croisy seem little disposed toward amorous rituals. They are justly critical of affectation, but they offer no truly positive example of proper courtship. Rather, their middle-class norms place them in a different value structure.

There is probably no truewit perspective in the play other than that inferred by the audience from so many examples of false wit and the satirical vantage point offered by the suitors. But the fact remains that the main explanation of false wit lies in geographical origin. These Précieuses are "pecques provinciales" (scene 1), refugees from the outer darkness of country life. They are ill-bred bourgeois counterparts of the Comtesse d'Escarbagnas. La Grange and Du Croisy underline from the beginning the comic clash between would-be refinement and grossly tactless conduct. The girls whisper to each other, yawn openly, rub their eyes, and otherwise mark the slow march of time inflicted upon them by such boring company (scene 1). It is this crass disregard for elementary politeness that the suitors are bent upon punishing and that they can explain only by the double effect of a metropolitan standard of taste too easily counterfeited and an ineradicable legacy of provincial life. The same causes account for the ease with which the girls are fooled by the "valet gentilhomme" Mascarille and his partner in engaging deception, Jodelet. Nothing can remedy these faults, for ineptitude cannot be erased or fine manners learned. Although the denouement points no further than comeuppance, the ladies must either return to their former backwoods life or remain perpetually vulnerable to new humiliations in a discerning capital. In Molière's second satire of provincial intrusion, *Monsieur de Pourceaugnac,* the antithesis with Paris mores is more clearly particularized. We do not know the Précieuses' home province, but Pourceaugnac expressly is a Limousin. He is a country knight as well, an *hobereau* like Monsieur de Sotenville but one who has made the mistake of uprooting himself. His aspirations to Paris authenticity are underlined in his costume (no. 21), a preposterously exaggerated version of the standard *galant* uniform complete with plumed hat, *justaucorps,* frilly neckwear, *haut-de-chausses,* and high-heeled shoes with pretentious ribbons. That a garish display of color was part of this adornment we know from the *Inventaire*: the *haut-de-chausses* is red, the long coat blue, the garters green, the hat gray with a green feather, the cloak rose-colored (p. 367). An extravagant counterfeit of beribboned Parisian elegance, then, betrayed by every word and gesture. A cloud of doubt, moreover, hangs over his claimed *noblesse d'épée.* He himself professes to have studied law (1. 3) and later shows suspicious familiarity with legal jargon: "quand il y aurait information, ajournement, décret, défaut et contumance" (etc.) (2. 10). But when it is suggested that he is "du métier," he denies any professional taint. He does not even admit to *la noblesse de robe:* "Je suis gentilhomme," he declares firmly and ascribes his legal competence to "le sens commun." He is reminiscent in this regard of Widow Blackacre, a *plaideuse* forming the subplot of Wycherley's *The Plain Dealer.* The Widow too is from the provinces (Norfolk) and steeped in legal cant: "The Fitz enters upon the Pere; and the Ayle brings his writ of disseisin in the *post* and the Pere brings his write of disseisin in the *per* and . . ." (1. 1). To be sure, she is not noble; but the stain of professionalism is linked, as in the case of Pourceaugnac, with country life.

Whereas the Précieuses have elected Paris as the site of a new life in general, Pourceaugnac's motivation is more limited: he has arrived to carry out his intention of marrying Julie, a Paris gentlewoman. The incongruity of this enterprise is underlined by Julie's maidservant, Nérine, in an expostulation to her mistress: "Une personne comme vous est-elle faite pour un Limousin? S'il a envie de se marier que ne prend-il une Limousine et ne laisse-t-il en repos les chrétiens?" (1. 2). This incongruous association of religious and worldly orthodoxy only reinforces the play's message: intruders are social heretics deserving of civil excommunication. Thus Pourceaugnac becomes the butt of a series of stratagems contrived to drive him back to his home province. The slapstick stunts that follow neutralize any fellow feeling one might direct toward him. The genre conventions of farce put him on the same level as the circus clown shedding mock tears after a series of pratfalls. And in terms of reigning social values, he is, of course, in the wrong. This pretender is all the more ludicrous because of the mediating truewit perspective found here and lacking in *Les Précieuses ridicules*. The wellborn Julie and her gallant Eraste, aided by the tricky valet Sbrigani and his accomplice Nérine, not only form the nucleus of the plot but also embody the high spirits, the youthful inventiveness, and the legitimate aspirations of young love as favored by the Paris elite represented in comedy.

Molière wrote no other comedy whose main purpose was to contrast Town manners with provincial backwardness. We have thus analyzed a fairly limited aspect of his comic art; but as we shall see in the coming chapter, he chose to develop other facets of the truewit/falsewit dialectic. An overview of Restoration manners comedy reveals a similarly restricted use of this geographical antithesis. Provincials comprise relatively few of the personages we see on stage. London characters, whether Town or City ones, were sufficient to carry out the comic purpose of Restoration playwrights. Yet, witticisms at the expense of country folk recur often, and in like manner Molière made passing allusions to uncouth behavior associated with a country upbringing. Valets, for instance, tend to claim a province as their home and indeed often carry that province or city as their name: Basque, La Flèche, and so on. In one memorable case, however, Molière stresses provincial birth as part of the strategy by which he devalues one of his most vividly drawn characters, Tartuffe. So compelling is the hypocrite's personality as it develops before our eyes that some indicators contributed by those around him fade into the background. The fact is, however, that he is a country boor aping Town manners, especially in his effort to play *l'honnête homme amoureux*. Not only is he a churl but one who claims noble status. "Il est bien gentilhomme," asserts Orgon (v. 494)—that is, a member of the *noblesse d'épée*. Yet Damis labels him a "pied plat," a man who wears (or should wear) the flat shoes of the lower social strata. These indices tend to slip by modern audiences, but Moliére could have inserted them to help deflect some of the virulent criticisms directed against the play. A provincial fraud would be viewed differently from a metropolitan man of the cloth, and his speech and actions would be commensurately devalued. An intruding adventurer refusing to acknowledge his true place, "il se méconnaît," to paraphrase Dorine's apt remark (v. 65). Thus when Tartuffe pursues his gross courtship and indulges in his spiteful scheming, we are to remember that he has come from the provinces to foist himself upon the scintillating life of Paris. The Sun King himself and his "vives clartés" (v. 1919) send him back to the shadows.

CAPITAL LACKWITS

If provincial origin is an indelible stain, being a native of the capital is no greater a guarantee of success in *le beau monde*. The inclusion/exclusion dialectic operates in Paris and also in London, since false wit is equally widespread there. In Restoration comedy we find two categories of false wit characters from the capital. The witwouds—those hangers-on who try vainly to emulate the code they see at work around them—and the witless, so far removed from *bel air* capabilities or so hostile to prevailing norms that they are permanent "outsiders." It is worth restating in this context the useful distinctions made by Aristotle in his *Nicomachean Ethics* (see p. 49): the "witty person" forms a happy mean between the two extremes of intemperate clowning and boorish, antisocial behavior. Unlike the outsider, however, the buffoon contributes to the spirit of good fun; the churl will have no part of it, being, in contrast to the high spirits and indulgence of the clown, judgmental and censorious. Such lively maidservants, for example, as Dorine, Nicole, and Toinette energize the atmosphere of their respective comedies (*Tartuffe*, *Le Bourgeois gentilhomme*, and *Le Malade imaginaire*); they are allied as well to the truewits, with the result that their brazen conduct and fearless impudence are instantly forgiven.

In Restoration comedy the witwoud category can be easily delineated, since it is filled almost exclusively by the many fops, "pert coxcombs," and preening courtiers that populate the stage. In their aspiration to wit, they share in the program of refined jollity that manners comedy seeks to implement; but their inability to emulate true wit authentically and with grace makes them perpetual figures of fun, ever-fresh subjects of mockery. The bemused tolerance expressed by Lady Townley in Etherege's *The Man of Mode* (a truewit character as her name implies) summarizes the Town attitude: "Tis good to have an universal taste; we should love wit, but for variety be able to divert ourselves with the extravancies of those who want it" (3. 2).

It would be otiose to list all those in Restoration comedy who "want wit" in this way. The most characteristic is the hero of *The Man of Mode*, Sir Fopling Flutter. Though episodic (we see him for the first time in act 3 and only occasionally thereafter), his presence pervades the play. The early conversation among the gallants, Dorimant, Medley, and Young Bellair, anticipates the traits that will be confirmed later. This fop, "lately arrived piping hot from Paris, . . . was yesterday at the play, with a pair of gloves up to his elbows and a periwig more exactly curled than a lady's head newly dressed for a ball" (1. 1). We learn that Sir Fopling has a "pretty lisp" learned from "the people of quality in France" and that "his head stands for the most part on one side, and his looks are more languishing than a lady's when she lolls at stretch in her coach or leans her head carelessly against the side of a box in the playhouse" (ibid.). True to his courting ways, "he has been . . . brisk upon the ladies already." The truewits summarize him as a "person . . . of great acquired follies, . . . like many others, beholden to his education for making him so eminent a coxcomb" (ibid.).

This portrait resembles more the sort of mincing Gallic effeminate that La Bruyère will ridicule in Iphis, the feyish courtier who tempts the author to place him in "le Chapitre des femmes,"[2] than the typical English fop of Restoration comedy. Yet the broad traits are there: extravagantly pretentious attire; studied, self-conscious gestures; derivative *galanterie*; a general air of self-satisfaction; and finally, the feature repeated from comedy to comedy, a woeful lack of personal authenticity. All is acquired, learned; his Gallomania has given him a hodgepodge of cultural poses, a veneer of cultivation that peels away at the slightest contact with superior wisdom, as when Sir Fopling confuses the fashionable French author Bussy-Rabutin with the sixteenth-century adventurer Bussy d'Amboise (4. 1).

Wycherley's fops are cast in the same mold. Sparkish of *The Country Wife* is categorized, again by the gallants, as "one of those nauseous offerers at wit, who, like the worst fiddlers, run themselves into all companies" (1. 1). Sparkish, true to form, invites himself along to dinner, demanding to have the company of genuine wits rather than be "with gay, shallow fops and silent coxcombs" (ibid.). In Wycherley's next play, *The Plain Dealer*, the fop appears in three varying guises: Novel, Major Oldfox, and My Lord Plausible are described in the dramatis personae as, respectively, "a pert, railing coxcomb and an admirer of novelties," a "an old impertinent fop, given to scribbling," and "a ceremonious, supple, commending coxcomb." Manly rages against Olivia's indulgence toward "these fluttering parrots of the town, apes and echoes of men only" (2. 1).

Similarly, Congreve depicts in *The Double Dealer* contrasting subtypes in Lord Froth, "a solemn coxcomb," and Brisk, "a pert coxcomb." But his more forgiving attitude toward human frailty comes through in the two delightful fops of *The Way of the World*, Witwoud and Petulant. Perpetually high-spirited, they compete in aphoristic brilliance. Mrs. Millamant disclaims having courted the favors of the *beau monde* in a recent promenade: "Oh I have denied myself airs today. I have walked as fast through the Crowd—" "As a favourite in disgrace," interjects Witwoud, "and with as few Followers." "Dear Mr. Witwoud, truce with your similitudes; for I am as sick of 'em—" "As a physician of a good air—I cannot help it Madam, tho' 'tis against myself," he chortles (1. 1).

Witwoud's conduct shows a prime trait of the fop: he lacks the self-awareness and sensitivity to know when he may be tolerated and when he is frankly insufferable. He breaks tactlessly into the witty sallies of the very lady he claims to be courting. He is impervious to reprimand; criticism rolls off his back, barbed jests are casually ignored. Conceit is indeed a hallmark of the type; he assumes that everyone thinks well of him. He is unable to make the distinction, crucial in that society, between conduct that shows a laudable personal style and that which betrays extravagant singularity. His clothing crosses the line from the clever touch to absurd ostentation. In short, he tries vainly to apply to his own person the standards that he imperfectly observes around him and that he can approximate only in a slapdash manner.

Yet he is tolerated in the circles he frequents. To be sure, he aspires to the same social program as that embodied in the truewit characters, and this very solidarity would allow for some indulgence. Of equal significance, his native good humor, his festive jollity contribute to the good fun that the wellborn make their chief pursuit in life. Sir Fopling aspires to the reigning social arts; he sings, dances, recites poetic homages to his lady; in act 2 he leads a round of drinking and happy song. Even Sparkish has a redeeming side in his irrepressible laughter. And we have just seen that Witwoud displays a similarly buffoonish spirit with his compulsive wit. We have here, in short, various versions of the harmless social butterfly tainted with no malice or vindictiveness. Vanity has not made them "sick with self-love," to borrow a phrase characterizing Malvolio in *Twelfth Night*, but rather entertaining, convivial presences. Were the fop truly perceptive, he would avoid the company he imitates so badly; but convinced as he is that he is in his rightful place, he pursues his pleasures with self-confidence and a thick skin, thus giving sport to those who, without his inanities, would have to be the exclusive architects of their own amusements.

Molière does not have recourse to the fop as often as do his fellows across the Channel, for whom the type conveys the most distinctive contrast between true and false wit. But the Frenchman was equally adept at caricaturing ill-conceived attempts to attain social brilliance. One of his first memorable roles, that of Mascarille in *Les Précieuses ridicules*, carries all the attributes of the preening coxcomb so well delineated in Restoration comedy. That he is a valet aping "l'homme de condition" is really of little consequence; the "marquis de Mascarille" will soon become in later incarnations a true holder of that rank. Since the fop is by definition a posturing, derivative fool acting a role for which he has no innate disposition, it matters little whether his fraudulence comes from an effort to rise to a higher social class or an attempt to validate the one to which he nominally belongs.

Brissart's engraving of 1682 highlights the ample signs of foppery that the audience would have recognized the moment Mascarille arrives on stage, even without the spectacular sedan-chair entry (no. 3). Hanging below the long coat (the *justaucorps*) with lavishly embroidered pockets—the prime sign of gentility—we note an ample tier of lace; enormous starched *canons* thrust out from the knees and almost reach the ankles. Neat ribbons stiffly decorate the dainty shoes, and the extravagantly plumed hat and fan-like flowing periwig complete the cluster of visual signs denoting the fop. The text itself alludes to this comic dress when Mascarille fishes for compliments about his "petite oie," his "canons," his perfumed gloves, and so on (scene 9). From an "habit de

marquis" for *Les Fâcheux* listed in the *Inventaire* we gain some ink-
ling as to the splashy colors that reinforced such vestimentary hyperbole: "un ringrave, avec une ample garniture d'incarnat et jaune
de colbertine, un pourpoint toile colbertine garnie de rubans, sou-
liers, bas de soie et jarretières" (p. 568). Such a gaudy display—
blue, pink, bright red, and yellow—was obviously calculated to
amuse.

Mascarille's conduct confirms our expectations. Without going into the obvious specifics—his cavalier treatment of the chair-
bearers, his extravagant courtship gestures, his poetry recitation—
we may summarize it all as simply a frenzied striving after wit. An
effort at clever repartee marks the very onset of the conversation
with Cathos and Magdelon. The labored metaphorical expression
of the witwoud reaches comic heights in dialogue like:

> MASCARILLE: Le mérite a pour moi des charmes si puissants que je
> cours partout après lui.
>
> MAGDELON: Si vous poursuivez le mérite, ce n'est pas sur nos
> terres que vous devez chasser.
>
> CATHOS: Pour voir chez nous le mérite, il a fallu que vous l'y
> ayez amené.
>
> [Scene 9]

Like Major Oldfox, Mascarille is "given to scribbling" and offers
us an example of his wit in the forced conceits of his "au voleur"
impromptu (ibid.).

The satirical charge carried by this farcical character does not
detract from the delightful spirit of buffoonery he embodies and to
which Jodelet can give only a rather feeble echo. When the *précieuses* marvel at his "caractère enjoué" (ibid.), they remind us that
the fop is engagingly fun-loving for all his shortcomings. Like Sir
Fopling, Mascarille yields easily to his high-spirited nature and
leads the dancing and singing climax to the play (scene 12). Indeed,
it would seem that Etherege had Mascarille in mind in many of the
comic effects he gives to his own man of mode.

The remaining fops in Moliére's theater are genuinely titled. The episodic Lysandre of *Les Fâcheux* (whose colourful costume is described in the *Inventaire* [p. 568]) is a man of rank, if we are to accept the excuse the hero Eraste offers for his own complaisance (vv. 209–12). Given the fact that the coxcomb "runs himself into all companies," to quote Wycherley, we should expect indeed to find him in this gallery of importunate people (tact being a specific quality of the elite). Lysandre is a would-be composer who insists on singing his latest ditty no less than five times in a row, after which he imposes a demonstration of the dance steps he has contrived to fit the music. As a final irritant, he forces Eraste to take the lady's part. Eraste parries the expected request for praise by such empty phrases as "tous ces pas-là sont fins." The most memorable aspect of Lysandre's characteristic conceit is expressed in words that Moliére was to take up in part later:

J'ai le bien, la naissance, et quelque emploi passable
Et fait figure en France assez considérable;
Mais je ne voudrais pas, pour tout ce que je suis,
N'avoir point fait cet air qu'ici je te produis.

[vv. 183–86]

Molière's next embodiment of the titled *bel-esprit* is the Marquis of *La Critique de l'Ecole des femmes*. We learn what to expect from him well before his arrival; Elise and Uranie, the discriminating *honnêtes gens* who together with Dorante form the exemplary center of the play, mock the "turlupinades perpétuelles" of this "marquis incommode." "La belle chose," declares Elise scornfully, "de faire entrer aux conversations du Louvre de vieilles équivoques ramassées parmi les boues des halles et de la place Maubert!" (scene 1). The Marquis's false wit is clearly stigmatized in class terms; unable to emulate the refined repartee of the king's court, this clown (Turlupin was one of the popular *farceurs* of the early seventeenth century) can resort only to the lowest forms of wordplay typical of the market district. Elise goes on to furnish a precise example of the Marquis's futile wit: "Qu'un homme montre d'esprit," she sneers, "lorsqu'il vient vous dire: 'Madame, vous êtes dans la Place Royale, et tout le monde vous voit de trois lieues de Paris, car chacun vous voit de bon oeil" (scene 1). The fop's compliment turns on a ponderous *calembour* alluding to Bonneuil, a village at a three-league distance from Paris. "Cela n'est-il pas bien galant et bien spirituel?" This mockery of the fop's false wit brings us remarkably close to the tone of Restoration comedy.

Once on stage, the Marquis confirms this advance billing. Thick-witted, opinionated, inarticulate (witness his repeated "détestable"), he is an object of our derision. Yet, his buffoonish energy brings the play to two separate heights of comic intensity: his madcap repetition of "tarte à la crème" in a crescendo of laughter and his braying song that puts an end to the parlor conversation remind us that the fop is an ally of the comic spirit and that his laughter, though commonly out of place and often tasteless, is laughter nonetheless.

No doubt this Marquis was dressed as extravagantly as Mascarille, although the fact that he is placed in a group portrait in the Brissart engraving (no. 9) draws attention away from him. We have a general impression of ostentation, but his costume is not that different from Dorante's, save that he is wearing his colorfully plumed hat. We are better able to see his successor in *L'Impromptu de Versailles* (no. 10), for we behold Molière at center stage and attired as the foppish Marquis whose role he is assuming in the dress rehearsal. Judging from the didactic gesture, Molière is probably taking momentarily Brécourt's role (that of the *honnête homme* Dorante) to emphasize the inexhaustible folly of mankind: "Attendez, il faut marquer davantage cet endroit . . . plus de matière?" (scene 4). Assuming that Brécourt is the character on our left, we can readily see a contrast between the fashionable dress of the truewit and the gaudy display of Molière's costume. Although not so flamboyant as Mascarille's, his attire carries clear indicators of exaggeration: an enormous wig, a *jabot* of majestic proportions, and the stiff ribbons on his shoes, the same that grace the footwear worn by Mascarille (no. 3) and by the province-grown pretender Pourceaugnac (no. 21). The shoes Brissart gives the young gallants, though delicately fashionable, are never so bedecked; only in Chauveau's 1661 engraving (no. 5) do we find an *amoureux* so adorned, in obvious obeisance to an earlier fashion. Fops with beribboned shoes thus betray out-of-date tastes when they are portrayed according to the vestimentary code of the 1680s. It would appear that the second marquis of the play (a role taken by La Grange) is not depicted by Brissart. But the two noblemen have an amusing conversation in scene 3 in which Molière satirizes the affected speech of the Marquis by reminding La Grange to assume it: "Bonjour, marquis"—"Mon Dieu, ce n'est pas là le ton d'un marquis; il faut le prendre un peu plus haut!"[3]

Molière's best-known coxcombs are those he represented in one of his acknowledged masterpieces, *Le Misanthrope*. Once again we see two *marquis*, Acaste and Clitandre, and another "homme de qualité," Oronte.[4] In creating the conceited Acaste, Molière seems to have remembered Lysandre from *Les Fâcheux*. Acaste's preening couplet "J'ai du bien, je suis jeune, et sors d'une maison / Qui se peut dire noble avec quelque raison" (vv. 783-84) is clearly reminiscent of Lysandre's own words quoted above. In fact, Lysandre seems to have split into two more fully developed types. The part of him that pretends to a fashionable composer becomes the poetaster Oronte, and Lysandre's song and dance, followed by compliment-fishing, is obviously the prototype of the sonnet scene of 1. 2. Clitandre's role is somewhat more subdued, although he joins Acaste in the salon scene in barbed comments intended to stimulate Célimène's disparaging wit. In his upbraiding of Célimène, Alceste himself satirizes Clitandre's foppish affectation in dress and gives us the same image in words as Brissart would have presented pictorially:

Vous êtes-vous rendue avec tout le beau monde
Au mérite éclatant de sa perruque blonde?

Sont-ce ses grands canons qui vous le font aimer?
L'amas de ses rubans a-t-il su vous charmer?
Est-ce par les appas de sa vaste rhingrave
Qu'il a gagné votre âme en faisant votre esclave?

[Vv. 481-86]

We remember that a *rhingrave* (an especially ample *justaucorps*) was listed for the *marquis* costume in *Les Fâcheux* and had thus become, no doubt—along with the outlandish *canons* and beribboned shoes—the main emblem of the fop.

The salon atmosphere of *Le Misanthrope*, the dominance of wit for wit's sake, usually at the expense of others, the characteristic spirit of emulation—all this brings us close to the essence of Restoration manners comedy. Another scene set in a similar locale brings up the same questions of wit and fashion, but in a very different context. The third act of *Les Femmes savantes*, Molière's last "belle comédie," perpetuates the drawing room atmosphere of *Le Misanthrope* and the caricatured form it had taken in *Les Précieuses ridicules*. However, Philaminte's circle of learned ladies aspires to a goal beyond accepted social practice. Rather than simply imitating norms badly, she and her coterie have rejected them altogether. They have set up not a bogus salon but an inward-looking "académie," a narcissistic, self-aggrandizing enclave established in a spirit of protest.

Yet their pretention to the undiscriminating accumulation of knowledge preserves the outward forms of salon behavior. Verbal cleverness is prized: "Qu'il a de l'esprit," exclaims Bélise of Trissotin (v. 725). Significantly, the pedant is not attired in the sober black of the learned man if we are to judge from the Brissart engraving (no. 23). Trissotin is shown dressed in the *justaucorps* worn by all the truewit gallants in Molière. On the other hand, he seems to be wigless and sporting a rather ordinary hat. Instead of the fashionable frilly *jabot*, he wears a simple collar like that found in the costume of Arnolphe and Tartuffe (nos. 8, 20). We note, moreover, none of the plumes and ribbons characteristic of elegant attire. In short, his clothing seems a hybrid of the ordinary and of flashy stylishness, a symbol of his own ambiguous social standing and the contradiction between his petty essence and his high-level pretentions. It is no coincidence that his costume so closely resembles that worn by George Dandin (no. 17).

Moreover, Trissotin plays the fop to foolish admirers of a drawing-room *galanterie* completely at odds with feministic demands. The banter exchanged between the ladies and the foppedant is as pretentious and banal as that of *Les Précieuses*:

PHILAMINTE: A notre impatience offrez votre épigramme.

TRISSOTIN: Hélas! c'est un enfant tout nouveau-né, Madame.
Son sort assurément a lieu de vous toucher.
Et c'est dans votre cour que j'en viens
d'accoucher.

PHILAMINTE: Pour me le rendre cher, il suffit de son père.

TRISSOTIN: Votre approbation lui peut servir de mère.

[Vv. 719-24]

Not only does he purvey a sonnet of rare triteness in a ludicrous effort reminiscent of the Bonneuil play on words in *La Critique de l'Ecole des femmes*, but Trissotin's *chute* for his subsequent epigram collapses miserably on the pedestrian *calembour* "amarante" / "de ma rente." So pleased is he with this conceit that he repeats the offending couplet.

Trissotin's desire to amuse in society, his outward acceptance of salon form, his exaggerated dress with its partial homage to fashion—all this makes him essentially a more serious variant of the fop, without, however, the redeeming buffoonery that makes the type tolerable. Trissotin is more a slave to rampant egoism than a guileless pretender to wit. Indeed, he is a *pharmakos* figure at the end of the play and thus anticipates the kind of character to be studied in the next chapter.

Chapter 5

THE WAGES OF INCIVILITY:
THE OUTSIDER FIGURE

If comedy in general validates a social bond, manners comedy, with its stress on contemporary mores, is yet more explicit in its effort to bring audience and spectacle into unspoken agreement about a specific social vision. And since the genre relies for its impact on strong polarities, we can readily expect the portrayal not only of more or less exemplary social behavior but also of conduct that transgresses or denies accepted norms. This negative side of the picture is always positive by implication; we recall Morel's apt image: "La caricature présente comme la moule en creux de l'honnête homme" (p. 116). The playwright gives clear signals that orient our reactions of scorn or mockery, and we quickly find ourselves sharing attitudes of opprobrium voiced by characters on stage. The attendant sense of complicity forms a clear bond with those embodying the positive pole.

Those who voice or exemplify precepts that fly in the face of accepted social practice we have called outsiders. The term as thus used denotes more a kind of cultural alienation than outright ostracism. The nay-sayer forms part of a complex dramatic and comic pattern; he is still a part of the social fabric and may indeed dominate in an authority structure: Molière's heavy fathers, for instance. But in general Molière's outsiders are not at home in the comic world, in the hedonistic, devil-may-care, spontaneous mood that vitalizes the genre. They reflect in general a reproving, solemn, moralistic view of the world. This attitude may have a surface respectability; however, the playwright is careful to undermine any positive basis for a killjoy attitude. In Orgon's case a moralistic attitude may take the proportions of gross inhumanity and vindictiveness. Often the outsider, in his contempt for present-day mores, is made to embody anachronistic values; witness Alceste's admiration of the good old days of heroic sincerity and authentic love songs. Or he may carry in himself a contradiction that invalidates his own precepts: a censorious attitude to *galanterie* may hide a festering sensuality and demeaning envy—the prudes on both sides of the Channel are invariably depicted as hypocrites.

Such types often are treated with a cruelty that seems a throwback to the pharmakos ritual. Comedy seems to reflect the need in society for a scapegoat around which to build its own sense of purity and righteousness. Jacques in *As You Like It* recognizes the incompatibility of his own melancholia with the "dancing measures" of festive society and, like Alceste, takes voluntary leave of it; but Malvolio is baited and hounded in *Twelfth Night* to a degree that seems unconscionable, however trying his vain and carping temperament. In Restoration comedy a comparable fate befalls the superannuated coquette, a butt of ridicule, deception, and mockery that has no equal measure with her all-too-human peccadillos. In Molière, characters like George Dandin and Monsieur de Pourceaugnac call up similar reactions. What have they done to have such punishment meted out, other than be their own gross and unperceptive selves? But such a standard of equity cannot be meaningfully applied to comedy. The outsider is punished simply because he is not an insider. To show the rightness of a particular social vision, the genre needs more than the affirmation of a code through precept or exemplariness; a strong antithesis must be put in place and endowed with a sufficient cluster of negative moral traits to make the outcome seem equitable.

We may conveniently subdivide the outsider figure into four subspecies. First we meet the boor pure and simple, that type defined by Aristotle as having no social use whatsoever. Here the antisocial character exists in his simplest state; he wants nothing of the world around him and holds to a singular ethos that is perceived as tainted with alien values or invalidated by a rampant egoism. Here we find Molière's *bons bourgeois* (e.g., the Sganarelle of *L'Ecole des maris*), or in English comedy, the boorish knight or citizen. Sometimes, however, the outsider, though still churlish in his essence, may have social pretentions, a desire to seize some of the attributes of exemplary society even if his nature or class origin make such aspirations absurd. Here we run the gamut from Monsieur de la Souche to Monsieur Jourdain in the *bourgeoisie parvenante*, and Alceste in the upper-class world. A special third kind of social ineptitude in both Restoration comedy and Molière is reserved for the aging coquette: her desires urge her toward conformity in the rituals of courtship, but her age, spiteful temperament, and affected character combine to keep her at a distance from the truewit center. Finally, Molière in particular makes much use of the learned pomposity of the professional. Here at the antipodes of "le bel air des choses" we find a fourth variant of the outsider: the doctors in particular, with whom we may classify other specialists and their pedantic display.

In Restoration comedy boors come quite naturally from the groups set in contrast with the Town. In addition to the bumpkin from the provinces, the citizen—the merchant from the City—is depicted as incapable of refinement, a slave to a churlish and possessive temperament. He is usually an offstage presence, either confined to his City or reported to have intruded into the Town. When he appears, it is often to bear the stigma of trade: thus in *The Plain-Dealer* an alderman is satirized for the "forfeitures, usury and extortion" that he innocently passes off as an "honest turning of the penny." A social climber as well, he covets a country estate that an impoverished young nobleman is forced to sell (3. 1). Thus the "city rogue" has little to recommend him, and scorn showered upon the London middle class is no different from the contempt with which the Paris burgher is treated in Molière.

As part of this caricature, fear of cuckoldry in Molière is invariably shown as an ignoble trait symptomatic of a middle-class mediocrity and one that brings the very dishonor it seeks to escape: the *barbons* of the two *école* plays, Sganarelle and Arnolphe, spring of course to mind. The London citizen is likewise ridiculed through unflattering quips: "Sure I was born with budding antlers, like a young satyr or a citizen's child" (*The Way of the World*, 3. 3). As Nicoll induces from such jibes, "the citizen's wives made fair game for the debauched sparks; their husbands were butts for ill-placed wit and buffoonery" (p. 8). The Pinchwife of Wycherley's *Country Wife* is the very emblem of the citizen-type: his callous behavior and jailer-like vigilance only play into Horner's hands and make the innocently sensual Margery yet more eager for extramarital consolation.

Restoration comedy inveighs against titled churls, too. As we saw, the apex of incivility is reached by Sir John Brute, the loathsome knight-husband of Vanbrugh's *The Provok'd Wife*. A carouser given to dubious company—we remember that his companions in revelry are Lord Rake and Colonel Bully—his boorish conduct passes all bounds. After feigning to be a parson during a drunken brawl, he returns home to force his attentions on his wife but falls into a snoring stupor before he can carry out his designs. In short, Vanbrugh has drawn the very character of the brutish male.

We find a less contemptible variant in the untitled "country blockhead," Sullen, from Farquhar's *Beaux' Stratagem*. A drunkard too, he is a man of few words, civil or no. He utters only what is required to communicate a message: the verbal embroidery implicit in polite discourse is unknown to him. The wives of both these characters are predictably wooed by gallants whose seductiveness, wit, and spark are all the more effective, given their ladies' matrimonial plight. George Dandin's dictatorial and brutal treatment of his wife places him in the same category, but his dominant identity as a would-be, a peasant nobleman, separates him from the Brutes and the Sullens, who aspire to no higher station.

The closest approximation in Molière to the full-fledged Restoration churl is the Sganarelle of *L'Ecole des maris*. His condemnation of prevailing social norms covers almost all areas of behavior, but finds its most vigorous expression in clothing. He rejects fashionable dress for himself and prefers the wise vestimentary uses of his "aïeux" (v. 74). This recourse to a bygone set of values is once again a sure sign of Otherness in manners comedy. Sganarelle tries to impose these austere ways on the younger generation as well; his ward, Isabelle, should wear "une serge honnête" (v. 117) instead of the attractive, modish dress in which Brissart actually represents her (no. 6). His preoccupation with attire is almost obsessive: he sneers at his brother's efforts to respect contemporary fashions and applauds a new (and ultimately futile) set of sumptuary laws (2. 7). All these allusions must have had special comic force given the costume that Brissart depicts for *him* in the same engraving. We see here the "comic uniform"[1] that Molière used for all his Sganarelle roles, a costume more that of a clown than of a representative of a specific social class: soft hat, ruff, short coat, breeches, flat shoes, and a cloak. We know from the *Inventaire* that the entire costume was the "couleur de musq" (p. 569), but some Sganarelle costumes were quite gaudy, such as the yellow and green one for *Le Médecin malgré lui* (ibid.). In any event, a character so dressed and pontificating so vehemently against current fashions must have been a subject of derision. Moreover, the resemblance to the first Sganarelle (no. 4), the eponymous hero of the popular one-act farce of the year before (1660), must have struck the audience; the memory of the earlier Sganarelle's clownish strutting and ludicrous obsession with cuckoldry were no doubt brought to collective awareness. In any event, Sganarelle's comic attire in *L'Ecole des maris* must have mitigated the loathing the spectator might have felt if he responded only to the text itself and its social implications. For Sganarelle's social program in every respect flies in the face of the "l'esprit du monde," and, without the comic devaluation effected by dress, could well be taken too seriously.

We find a similar global condemnation of *le bel air*, but by more episodic and two-dimensional characters, in the *bons bourgeois* of Molière's early farces. The Gorgibus of both *Les Précieuses ridicules* and *Sganarelle* share, besides their farcical name, the same narrow perspective on society, with no aspect of fashionable social practice finding grace in their eyes. Even if the *Précieuses* possessed the taste and judgment necessary to apply properly their program of high-flown emulation, their father would oppose their enterprise because he sees the world in terms of the mercantile values that Molière invariably derides. Not only is marriage a contract whereby daughters are exchanged for goods, but Gorgibus displays an accountant's mentality in totting up the price of the beauty displayed by the *Précieuses*: "Elles ont usé . . . le lard d'une douzaine de cochons pour le moins, et quatre valets vivraient tous les jours des pieds de mouton qu'elles emploient" (scene 3). The second Gorgibus, from *Sganarelle*, shares the same scorn for fashionable reading and urbane pursuits in general, but his hostility to "l'esprit du monde" is the more telling because it is directed at a young lady who is destined for a romantic union. Thus he attacks directly the social comportment to which Célie, his daughter, aspires and to which, unlike the *Précieuses*, she is entitled by virtue of character and breeding. The contrast between dour, heavy-handed authority and the hedonism of a fun-loving society is conveyed in literary terms: Gorgibus rejects the modish novel *Clélie* in favor of tedious cautionary tracts ("les *Quatrains* de Pybrac et les doctes *Tablettes* / du conseiller Matthieu" [vv. 33–43]), including a didactic treatise by a Dominican monk.

This kind of monolithic opposition to normal social practice also comes to the fore in three more fully fleshed outsider figures. In the case of two of them, Orgon and Argan, their thralldom to an antisocial role is the result, in part at least, of a powerful, intrusive force in the family. Orgon's rejection of all social commitments—indeed, of humankind altogether: "Et je verrais mourir frère, enfants, mère et femme, / Que je m'en soucierais autant que de cela" (vv. 278–79)—is the work of Tartuffe; when the impostor's influence is removed, Orgon's naturally sociable and humane attributes return, and he readily accepts the norms that his family has almost unanimously upheld during the play. In like manner Argan is mesmerized by his second wife, who plays a *pharmakos* role similar to Tartuffe's. Bélise imposes another kind of negative reign: by catering to Argan's hypochondria, she preserves the dangerous and antisocial presence of the doctors in the household. Her perfidious efforts to provoke a break between Argan and his daughter and thereby have the latter sent off to a convent attack the very basis of social renewal. Though Argan does not come to his senses in the same complete way as does Orgon, the removal of a baleful influence allows the truewits, led by Béralde, to contrive a benign strategem that restores the reign of festivity and social amusement: the mock ceremony by which Argan receives his M.D.

The Chrysale of *Les Femmes savantes* may seem at first to be misplaced in this category. Unlike the other two, he is on the right side of the lover plot from the beginning and deplores the intellectual excesses of his wife's Academy. But the ideal to which this learned salon of erudite females alludes parodically is the genuinely genteel circle where refined wit dominates and where conversation moves spontaneously and with ease from subject to subject without embarrassing ignorance or showy pedantry. The play itself points to such a mocking interpretation; we have seen how the ladies endeavor, through Trissotin's posturing, to inject an affected strain of *galanterie* into their labored strivings. However, nothing in what Chrysale says and does shows any allegiance to this implied social ideal. His is the extreme of anti-intellectualism; for him there is little cultural dimension to life. Creature comforts round out his vision of the perfect life: good food, a docile wife with only enough knowledge to tell the difference between a jacket and a pair of breeches ("A connaître un pourpoint d'avec un haut-de-chausse" [v. 579])—such is the down-to-earth program of this mild-mannered, ineffectual burgher. Thus, although not in open rebellion against the prevailing social code, he has no understanding of it and consequently no wish to emulate it in the slightest. His opposition to the learned ladies, though well-founded and laudable, does not make him a spokesman for the norm or its embodiment. Contrary to the logic often accepted in earlier scholarship, two opposing positions can be equally wrong and mediated in fact by a third implied one that the audience will readily decode.

Thus we see that Molière exploited with consummate skill the comic value of monomania, by definition a threat to a society needing imaginative and adaptable members. Whether the result of an alien influence or the character's own deficiency, the versions of the type run from the simpleminded cardboard caricatures of the *bon bourgeois* to the compelling stage presence of an Orgon or a Chrysale. But the playwright probably realized that yet greater comic value lay in the portrayal of outsiders who, instead of being wholly opposed in precept and example to the social norms of the time, affect general condemnation while at the same time cultivating some attributes of the society they decry. We find in operation then the principle of contradiction, of inconsistency, which Molière exploited with such mastery. This process has been at work in two of the provincial pretenders discussed earlier: Dandin rejects the most important single institution of polite society—*galanterie*—and imposes a churlish vision of human relationships founded on abusive authority and endless self-mortification; yet he longs to be accepted into a class for which such a demeaning way of life would be unthinkable. Similarly, the French country knight Pourceaugnac devalues his claim to rank by a professional taint running through his pretended *gentilhommerie* and by the unseemly fear and doltish confusion he betrays in his Paris adventure.

Four of Molière's most memorable creations belong to this category of outsider pretender: Arnolphe, Harpagon, Monsieur Jourdain, and Alceste. The protagonist of *L'Ecole des femmes* bears a strong resemblance to his counterpart in the previous *école* play. Although Arnolphe pays less attention to dress, his concept of social and marital life, as well as the grotesque fears that feed it, is reminiscent of what we have already seen in Sganarelle. But one attribute of social custom survives this wholesale rejection: aristocratic title and the prerogatives and self-importance it gives. That the name Monsieur de la Souche is a fraudulent affectation is evident throughout the play; a genuinely titled person would have more regard for all the aspects of fashionable life decried by Arnolphe: "femmes habiles," "ruelles," and the like. The *bourgeois* may be able to live nobly, but to embody nobility is another matter. It is noteworthy that, although Arnolphe is usually decked out like a fop in modern productions of the play (e.g., the ostentatious hat, wig, and splendid longcoat worn by Louis Jouvet in the photographic records of his productions of *l'Ecole des femmes*), the character is shown in both the Chauveau and the Brissart engravings dressed in sober bourgeois attire (e.g., no. 8). The costume is not described in the *Inventaire*, but it must have been similar to the dark middle-class dress worn by Orgon and Harpagon if we can judge from the costumes noted in the same document. The Miser's costume was, in part, "un manteau, chausse et pourpoint de satin noir, garni de dentelle ronde de soie noire"; items for Orgon's dress included "pourpoint, chausse et manteau de vénitienne noire" (p. 567). The *pourpoint*, or short coat, was, we recall, the lower-class counterpart to the *justaucorps*, the flashy long coat sported by the gallants of the gentry. The costumes worn by Orgon and Harpagon were made of the finest materials, to be sure, but the stress laid on unrelieved blackness needs no emphasis. Social pretense, then, was meant to clash with outward appearance as well; Arnolphe's preening smugness is a parodic form of aristocratic pride and out of place in the social milieu denoted by his costume.

It is widely agreed that Harpagon is not a classic miser wallowing in his chest of gold coins and oblivious to all else save acquiring yet more. Molière's *avare* seems to be guided by a kind of *gageure*, a self-fashioned challenge to emulate as much of the upper-class way of life as may be consistent with spending little or no money. Thus this able-bodied man, whose sturdy legs should suffice for locomotion were he a full-fledged miser, sports horses and carriage, important status symbols in the gentry; but his steeds are dying of hunger. He keeps livery and domestic servants, even if he makes some of his *maisonnée*, like Maître Jacques, do double duty as cook and groom. He tries to conform not only with the material signs of status but also with the most important ritual of polite society: courtship. His conduct toward Mariane in 3. 5 is, of course, ludicrous; but his forced compliments, his vain self-rejuvenation bear witness to the pretentions of a would-be, a fop who would participate in the life of true gallants. But a fop, being usually titled, has at least some claim to a place in polite society, whereas Harpagon's affectations fail to hide a churlish nature exacerbated by a grasping disposition.

The contradiction is rendered once again on the level of costume. The miser scorns the very dress that a courting male would wear: "Il est bien nécessaire," he sneers to his son, "d'employer de l'argent à des perruques, lorsque l'on peut porter des cheveux de son cru?" (1. 4). The engraving for *L'Avare* (no. 18) conveys the same contrast Brissart rendered so often between dark sobriety (or clownish motley) associated with the eccentric and the colorful, elegant dress worn by the young suitor, Valère in this case. We recall that Harpagon is attired in black, and the engraving shows his *intendant* with a plumed hat, wig, and *justaucorps*—all signs of the truewit gallant. (The *Inventaire* indicates a "perruque" as well, but it could not have been part of Molière's costume for Harpagon, since the above quotation about "cheveux de son cru" indicates the contrary; the criticism would have no meaning if the miser himself were wearing a wig).

Finally, it must not be forgotten that Harpagon is a living betrayal of his station, as his son rightfully tells him: "Ne rougissez-vous point de déshonorer votre condition par les commerces que vous faites?" Cléante exclaims during their bitter confrontation in 2. 4. Harpagon is indeed the only character in Molière who, while living nobly, continues to amass wealth through mercantile pursuits, including the most demeaning one of lending for exorbitant interest. Thus the costume of a proper landed bourgeois is in itself a fraudulent sign.

Monsieur Jourdain is the one outsider whose sole objective is to get inside. Through the acquisition of wit, he hopes to join the *honnêtes gens* and their sparkling conversation and leave his former state behind forever. Out of a complex, subtle code of external indices (dress, hairstyle, language, social world, etc.) and inward qualities like judgment and discretion, all made effortlessly manifest by the elite, Jourdain closes in with a heavy hand on the most obvious, without being able to take into account the delicate interrelationships implied in correct social practice, especially the need to reconcile a certain personal style within the taste norms of the group. Thus stylish individualism becomes for Jourdain mere garish ostentation; his successive costumes, in their hilarious gaudiness, make one think of the affected coxcomb. But once again, the fop is an habitué, often titled, with enough polish to deserve to a certain degree his place in the Town or in the salons. For that reason foppery is normally not associated with upward mobility. What with all his pretentions, Jourdain remains an outsider. It is worth stressing that Jourdain does not carry his pretentions to other venues, other social circles, as would a proper coxcomb. By his lavish spending, he brings a facsimile of fashionable life to his own house, and the masters required to teach him the ways of the gentry are careful to insulate his narcissistic world against deflation, even to the very end. Although happily unaware of the fact, Jourdain has failed to grasp a cardinal rule of the genteel life: a man of quality is born, not made. If an aspirant has to *learn* the rules, his efforts must prove fraudulent and fruitless.

Nowhere is this more evident than in Jourdain's cult of the Lady. The gibberish of the *billet doux* to his *marquise,* his bumbling compliments, his botched *révérence,* his unremitting buffoonery, constitute a hilarious parody of *galanterie* (3. 16 to 4. 1). Indeed, by his unwitting allegiance to the principle of fun, he once again makes us think of the fop and his amiable high spirits. But the coxcomb has enough wit to counterfeit it with a modicum of success. In *Le Bourgeois gentilhomme* as in no other play, Molière shows the contrast between hopeless aping and festive worldliness, embodied especially in Dorante's distinction and flair. A well-rounded, intricate art of living becomes in Jourdain's clumsy hands a mindlessly uncoordinated choice among dimly understood social indices.

A word must be said about Madame Jourdain in this context. Her scorn for her husband's affectations does not, of course, make her a truewit. She is yet more of an outsider than Monsieur Jourdain because she supports unabashedly the world of the City, the mercantile values and self-satisfaction of *la bonne bourgeoisie*, and refuses to respect in any way the courtly values being projected into her house. Her humorless and reproving temperament clashes with any festive mood built up in the play, whether in the churlish interruption of the banquet (4. 2) or in her obstinate refusal to enter the spirit of innocent deception that marks the end of the comedy. In a sense she is a boor figure like the Sganarelle of *L'Ecole des maris*, with the important difference that she supports at least one group of truewits, the young lovers Cléonte and Lucile.

So far we have dealt with outsider figures who, whatever their degree of pretentiousness, belong to a lower social stratum signified by their costume. When the spectator first sees Arnolphe's *bourgeois* dress, or Jourdain's absurdly tasteless motley, he makes a judgment that will govern his attitude and expectations during the whole play. When, however, at the beginning of *Le Misanthrope*, two young blades appear on stage, both almost identically dressed in all the finery associated with upper-class life, we expect equal respect for, and embodiment of, proper social practice. It is clear from iconographical evidence that no significant contrast was intended between Philinte's costume and Alceste's. An anonymous engraving of 1667 (no. 13) represents only minor differences in apparel—Philinte's larger and more decorated hat, the ribbons on his shoes. Otherwise both wear the upper-class male uniform: a flowing, frilly *justaucorps* almost covering ample *haut-de-chausses*, high-heeled shoes, an elegant *jabot* at the neck, a copious periwig, and a sash slung diagonally across the torso and supporting a sword (the point of Alceste's weapon is visible next to his right calf). Brissart's engraving shows a much more revealing difference in gesture and attitude between the two men (no. 14), but again the two costumes are virtually the same, the chief difference being, once more, the hat. The description of Alceste's costume in the *Inventaire* gives some idea of the sumptuous materials and colors that accompanied these elegant forms: "haut-de-chausses et justaucorps de brocart rayé or et soie gris, doublé de tabis, garni de ruban vert, la veste de brocart d'or, les bas de soie et jarretières" (p. 568).

The text confirms Alceste's beribboned elegance, for Célimène herself labels him "l'homme aux rubans verts" (v. 1690). Two elegant gentlemen, then. But only one turns out to be a man of the world; the other impresses us from the start as, to speak oxymoronically, a courtly boor. At the very beginning of the play, by an adroit manipulation of visual signs, Molière plunges us straightaway into the unsettling ambiguities of his greatest masterpiece. The world view conveyed by the play as a whole comes remarkably close to the cynical urbanity of the Restoration. Neither Philinte nor Célimène, nor Alceste for that matter, has any illusions about mankind. They all see society as a jungle of conflicting egos where one's own self-interest must reign supreme. The debate revolves around the stance to take before this state of affairs. Célimène blithely applies the rampant *amour-propre* of Hobbesian natural man to civilized society. She revels in adulation, triumphs in witty backbiting, carefully preserves good relations with influential friends. In all this, as well as in other respects detailed earlier (pp. 72–73), she is not vastly different from the Restoration gentlewoman, a truewit in her own way. In the more forgiving atmosphere of Restoration comedy, her peccadillos would be the object of indulgent laughter, and a twist would reestablish her ascendancy and happy prospects for the future. Molière situates us more in the ambience of the animal fable and its harsher concept of comic justice; Célimène has overreached herself and deserves the setback she suffers, if only temporarily, at the end.[2]

In their attitude toward the failings of mankind, Philinte and

Eliante represent the exemplary center of *Le Misanthrope*. While recognizing man's basic rapacity, they show the kind of thoughtful, outward-looking behavior by which civilized custom masks and blunts the aggressiveness of "le moi qui se veut tout." They pinpoint clearly the irreconcilability between absolute truth and social practice, both in Philinte's conversation with Alceste at the beginning of the play and in Eliante's set piece showing how love transforms all to its idealizing image (vv. 711–30). In a word, they embody the shaky truce implicit in civility.

Alceste would strip away the pretense of civilized behavior and its inevitable hypocrisy to reveal the harsh law of the self, and the self in its most immediate and compelling form, himself. This surface dogmatism and absoluteness hides a narcissistic preoccupation. But the contradictions of his behavior do not lie solely in a general attitude toward the self in society. His ambivalence to the norms of his own upper-class world is only too evident. As we have just seen, he wears not only the costume of a young gallant but an especially sumptuous one—clothing hardly consistent with a vocation for misanthropy or for a possible solitary life with his beloved. This here-and-now dress is still less fitting for someone whose world view seems to hark back to an earlier mythical era of rectitude: "cette grande roideur des vertus des vieux âges," as Philinte puts it (v. 154). He not only looks the part of an urbane *honnête homme* but even appears to be a social gadabout, or at the very least an habitué of Célimène's circle. Although his courtship takes an inverted, querulous form, it is nonetheless courtship; and his profession of absolute sincerity, when put to the test with Oronte, breaks down into deft, civilized circumlocution. Though he despises backbiting, his scathing *caractère* of Clitandre (vv. 475–88) outdoes in its hostility any of Célimène's raillery, and with more passion than wit. In short, while inveighing against the social niceties of his time, while deploring man's duplicity and insincerity, this upper-class melancholic continues to play the game, oblivious to the inconsistencies of his own attitudes and unable to accept with humor and resignation the frailties of human nature. No better comic illustration of our love-hate relationship with our own kind has been staged.

So far in this chapter, we have been concerned in general with the great adversarial forces in Molière, the domineering naysayers who stand in opposition to the norms of social practice implicit and explicit in his theater. The heavy father and his surrogates project in general an out-of-date world view and try to force it upon the young by the weight of their legal authority. Usually their efforts meet with failure, and proper, present-day social practice emerges triumphant, whether by powers within or without the dramatic fabric.[3] This pattern, so distinctive in Molière, constitutes the major difference between him and Restoration comedy. Occasionally spokesmen for eccentric values appear, but their presence is episodic. Sir Sampson Legend, a father figure in Congreve's *Love for Love*, is a pleasant humor character with an obsessive interest in astrology; he is tricked at the end so that true love can be consummated, but he has no dominant or central role in the play. In *The Beaux' Stratagem* we meet Lady Bountifull, "an old civil country gentlewoman" respecting quaint provincial standards of politeness but posing no threat to the truewits. Lady Woodvill, a character in *The Man of Mode*, is categorized as "a great admirer of the forms and civility of the last age" (the reign of James I) (1. 1). Since she has dominance over her daughter, Harriet, a gentlewoman courted by Dorimant, the latter must cater to her old-fashioned prejudices and draw out such nostalgic dictums as "Lewdness is the business now; love was the business in my time" (4. 1). Lady Woodvill could have been a kind of heavy mother, but her role is a small one, and she is quickly won over at play's end.

Lady Woodvill's censorious remark reminds us of a type that did have wide currency in Restoration comedy, the superannuated coquette discussed in chapter two. If there is a foil to Restoration truewits comparable in function to the Molière characters commented upon thus far in the present chapter, it is the *femme galante* in the mold of Lady Cockwood, Mrs. Loveit, Lady Wishfort, and the like. Normally without effective legal power over other characters, they tend to interfere with the course of true love by scheming, backbiting, and treachery. Their lubricious nature underscores the relative decorum of the young gentlewomen, and their affected emphasis on outward form emphasizes by contrast the naturally genuine and gracious conduct of exemplary personages. Lady Wishfort is constantly wary lest she make a "prostitution of decorums" and protests her innocence to a suitor: There is not "the least scruple of carnality" in her conduct (*The Way of the World*, 4. 1). Further, their humorless, critical stance in the face of alleged immorality turns them into killjoys. Thus Wycherley's Olivia in *The Plain Dealer*, who will later try virtually to rape a young spark (who turns out to be Manly's devoted lady Fidelia), expresses sheer nausea over the "filthy play" *The Country Wife*, which Wycherley, emulating Molière,[4] cleverly slips into the discussion. So outraged does she profess to be over the notorious "china scene" that she is tempted to "break all my defil'd vessels. . . . Filthy china; nasty, debauched china!" (2. 1). The clash between such surface virtue and deep, unbridled sensuality creates here the most hilarious of comic incongruities.

Thus the combination of an advancing age that augurs ill for continuing affairs of the heart and the kind of festering, spiteful temperament one can expect from outward moral zeal, fevered blood, and an often crushed ego makes of the old coquette a powerful figure in Restoration comedy. Although Molière had less overall recourse to the type and was bound to standards of theatrical decorum that lessened perforce her satirical impact—he could not show forth her lust in the same crude terms as Wycherley did—he sometimes adds to prudish behavior a dimension absent in its Restoration counterpart. The frustrated coquette depicted by Molière takes refuge not only in spurious decorum but in devout behavior. Thus, by outward religious practice, she hopes to authenticate her pretenses. This link between *pruderie* and *dévotion* will be a distinctive feature of the type after Molière.

The prude appears, to begin with, in several *caractères* scattered throughout his theater. Uranie, in *La Critique*, recounts the squeamish reactions of several ladies at a performance of *L'Ecole des femmes*; so affected was their outward mien that a lackey "cria tout haut qu'elles étaient plus chastes des oreilles que de tout le reste du corps" (scene 3). In *Tartuffe* Dorine expands wittily on the demeanor of Orante, the family's hypercritical neighbor, whose every thought supposedly is on Heaven ("tous ses soins vont au Ciel"):

> Il est vrai qu'elle vit en austère personne;
> Mais l'âge dans son âme a mis ce zèle ardent,   p, /6
> Et l'on sait qu'elle est prude à son corps défendant.
>
> [Vv. 122–24]

In short, we behold but "les retours des coquettes du temps":

> Il leur est dur de voir déserter les galants.
> Dans un tel abandon leur sombre inquiétude
> Ne voit d'autres recours que le métier de prude.
>
> [Vv. 131–34]

The same satiric spirit gives force to Célimène's portrait of Arsinoé, whose "triste mérite, abandonné de tous, / Contre le siècle aveugle est toujours en courroux" (vv. 859–60).

Prudes appear on stage as well. Climène proves the veracity of Uranie's anecdote when she appears in *La Critique* to fulminate against the obscenities of *L'Ecole des femmes* (a scene Wycherley probably had in mind when he has Olivia condemn *The Country Wife*); her studied walk, pursed mouth, and languid voice only make her extreme reactions yet more ludicrous. The most memorable onstage prude, however, is Arsinoé, Célimène's spiteful enemy. Her conduct confirms what we have already been told. Her perfidious, self-righteous nature comes out in the dressing-down she gives Célimène; but all pretense is torn away when this high-principled lady invites Alceste to her quarters to offer him "de quoi [le] consoler" (v. 1131). Her behavior is all the more ludicrous in that she affects high religious principle:

> Elle est à bien prier exacte au dernier point;
> Mais elle bat ses gens et ne les paye point.
> Dans tous les lieux dévots elle étale un grand zèle;
> Mais elle met du blanc, et veut paraître belle.
>
> [Vv. 939–42]

Such is Célimène's biting, and no doubt accurate, characterization.

Armande, the defender of spiritual values in Les Femmes savantes, carries, but in a more devious way, the same blend of professed virtue, underlying spite, and ill-contained sensuality. "Mariez-vous, ma soeur, à la philosophie" (v. 44) she admonishes her sister; and when the latter chooses instead to accept the man whom Armande has disdained, the would-be bride of learning can scarcely hide her rage. Later her lurking instincts spring into words with her rapturous "on se meurt de plaisir" (v. 810), aroused by the hearing of Trissotin's sonnet (3. 2).

What is especially significant in all this is that on both sides of the Channel comedy devalues prudishness as a negative and hypocritical attitude. There are no respectable, sincere prudes. Even Madame Pernelle, although genuinely preoccupied with moral questions and far beyond the age of carnality, is shown to be a fool in her hyperbolical, raging condemnation of peccadillos, her unfeeling treatment of her servant, whom she slaps with a "marchons, gaupe, marchons" (v. 171), and the stubborn blindness she shows in act 5 when everyone else is convinced of Tartuffe's perfidy. This prejudice may be explained, perhaps, by the ambiguous place of religion in seventeenth-century French society and the problem of portraying religious forms in a comic perspective. There is obviously a conflict between an official religion stressing man's soul and its afterlife and a society given to hedonistic self-indulgence, with the royal defender of the faith—a libertine punctilious in religious ritual—setting the prime example. Polite society, no matter how reasonable and refined, still values the *siècle* to the detriment of the life beyond. Comedy must come to terms with this permanent tension. A genuine profession of a spirituality hostile to the corporeal would be out of place, not only because comedy reflects such fundamental social rites as *galanterie* but also because the genre itself stresses the kind of physical and social renewal that would be impossible if the horror of the flesh were institutionalized. For that reason Molière avoids the sincerely religious or virtuous implications of prudishness; rather, he portrays fanatical devotion as something no reasonable man could condone: love of one's neighbor, for instance, is perverted into Orgon's vision of the human race as "fumier" (v. 274). It is Cléante's role to mediate for the spectator the conflict between this world and the other, to reconcile religious practice with the claims made upon social man.

The prude in comedy, then, is by definition a figure of ridicule. In her hypocritical refusal of the flesh and her frenzied if repressed libido, she embodies the contradictory extremes that the ardent but decorous suitors of comedy are meant to mediate. In no other character is this feature so apparent as in Molière's only male prude, Tartuffe. We have already noted his social pretentions, his claim to rank belied by every aspect of his character, including his provincial origin. Tartuffe's spurious prudishness in his first appearance reveals Molière's theatrical genius at its highest point. The sight of an audience ("*apercevant Dorine*") calls forth the histrion who first plays the self-mortifying saint: "Laurent, serrez ma haire avec ma discipline" (v. 853), then the zealot recoiling before carnal temptation: "Couvrez ce sein que je ne saurais voir" (v. 860). These concentrated effects, carefully prepared in earlier scenes, foreshadow the whole unveiling of Tartuffe's character, his explicit and unbridled sexuality (more appropriate to masculine decorum but still totally at odds with respectful courtship) and the studied way in which he preaches virtue. Dorine's anecdote about Taruffe's servant epitomizes best perhaps this reign of theatrical dissembling:

Il vient nous sermonner avec des yeux farouches
Et jeter nos rubans, notre rouge et nos mouches.
Le traître, l'autre jour, nous rompit de ses mains
Un mouchoir[5] qu'il trouva dans une *Fleur des Saints*,
Disant que nous mêlions, par un crime effroyable,
Avec la sainteté les parures du diable.

[Vv. 205–10]

We come now to the last insider/outsider dichotomy to be discussed, the opposition between professional specialization with its learned cant and the ideal of well-rounded, socially oriented knowledge and its pleasant and accessible mode of expression as summed up in the ideal of *honnêteté*. Molière exploited with consummate skill the rich comic potential of this *monde/université* polarity, especially in his portrayal of doctors. In Restoration comedy such contrasts, though by no means rare, do not constitute a major feature. Again, the stress seems to be on a consistent, balanced image of wit and its variations. Wycherley does, however, create a forceful caricature of the law-minded lady in the Widow Blackacre of *The Plain Dealer*. Like the litigious characters of Racine's *Les Plaideurs*, this would-be barrister knows of nothing but the courtroom. Her language is colored by her obsession. On the verge of being forced to marry Freeman, a young but impoverished gallant who covets her wealth, she tries to negotiate a compromise: "I am contented that you should hold and enjoy my person by lease or patent; but not the spiritual patent, call'd a license; that is, to have the privileges of a husband, without the dominion; that is, *durante bene placito*; in consideration of which, I will, out of my jointure secure you an annuity of three hundred pounds a year" (5. 1). Her use of rambling legalese to express a simple, straightforward conjugal arrangement is a good comic illustration of her mania. She tries, moreover, to instill the same litigious spirit in her son Jeremy, whom she orders to read lawbooks rather than frivolous plays.

Another English character whose mania drives him to a specialized jargon is Forsight, "an illiterate old fellow . . . pretending to understand Astrology, Palmistry, Physiognomy, Omens, Dreams, etc.," whom we find in Congreve's *Love for Love.* The text emphasizes jargon appropriate to these arcane disciplines, for example, his obsession with the first: "I have travell'd and travell'd in the celestial spheres, know the signs and the planets and their houses, can judge of motions direct and retrograde, of sextiles, quadrates, trines and oppositions, fiery trigons and aquatic trigons . . ." (2. 1).

Molière mocked similar types in *Les Fâcheux,* where *maniaques* of all kinds successively annoy Eraste: Alcippe, the inveterate gamester with his jargon (2. 2); Dorante, whose hunting vocabulary intrudes into everything he says (2. 6); Caratidès, a pedantic, long-winded prattler campaigning against badly written inscriptions (3. 2). But in general Molière dwells little on such harmless eccentrics, preferring no doubt to flesh out strong monomaniacal characters who can sustain an entire dramatic action.

Curiously enough, the legal profession and its archaic, Latinizing cant, a ready target for all satirists and the object of Racine's only comedy, is left relatively untouched by Molière. Only in three plays does a man of law appear, and then only episodically; two are mere notaries and the third a provincial *conseiller.* Thus no reference is made to the higher magistrature, like the judge so drolly caricatured by Racine. The first legal official to appear in Molière is the one summoned by Arnolphe in *L'Ecole des femmes* (4. 2). Arnolphe is too stunned by his misfortunes and the notary too absorbed in his professional role for anything but a dialogue of the deaf to result, laced with legal barbarisms:

> Et cela par douaire, ou préfix qu'on appelle,
> Qui demeure perdu par le trépas d'icelle.
> Ou sans retour, qui va de ladite à ses hoirs,
> Ou coutumier, selon les différents vouloirs
>
> [Vv. 1064–66]

The notary who advises Béline and Argan in *Le Malade imaginaire* (1. 7) shows a more sinister side of the trade: he is quick with stratagems to evade the spirit and the intent of the law. Interestingly enough, it is this notary, not a doctor, that Brissart portrays in his engraving for the play (no. 24)—evidence that this particular scene with a whimpering wife, a smugly self-assured professional, and an ingenuously moved hypochondriac had some lasting impact upon the audience. In *La Comtesse d'Escarbagnas*, the *conseiller* Thibaudier carries legal cant even into the refinements of courtship: speaking to the heroine concerning Julie, a lady who is supposed to be helping him win the Comtesse's heart, he promises that "si elle a jamais quelque procès en notre siège, elle verra que je n'oublierais pas l'honneur qu'elle me fait de se rendre auprès de vos beautés l'avocat de ma flamme" (scene 5).

If Molière largely spared men of law, it was only to turn yet more satiric fire upon another professional fraternity, the doctors. Thus Molière's most characteristic antithesis between *le bel air* and vapid learning is provided by the medical profession. We see them several times in the Brissart engravings, especially the four depicted in number 12: they wear, like the legal confraternity, the long black cloaks of their calling and stand thereby in visual opposition to the fashionably bedecked gallants. Basically they are variations of the timeless *dottore*-pedant of the *commedia dell'arte*, but Molière is careful to situate them in a historical present. Thomas Diafoirus displays, for instance, a thesis he has defended against "les circulateurs," those who uphold Harvey's contentions regarding the movement of blood in the body. By Molière's time the general conservatism and recourse to obsolete authority of Molière's doctors form an absurd anachronism setting off the here-and-now celebrated in manners comedy. Molière's caricatural verve spares no facet of the training undergone by future practitioners—especially the concentration on formal disputation described by Diafoirus *père* (2. 5) and exemplified by a parodic scene in *Monsieur de Pourceaugnac* (1. 8), or the inept application of their lore (such as in the several ludicrous consultations we witness here and there).[6] But his main satirical force underlines social ineptitude. The doctor is a permanent misfit, and his intrusion into polite society can result only in ridicule and humiliation. This message, implied whenever Molière touches on the profession, reaches its most hilarious expression in the self-conscious, pedantic formalism exemplified by young Diafoirus, so sharply contrasting with Cléante's fashionable little opera and his proper courtship of his beloved (*Le Malade imaginaire*, 2. 5). Once again we return to the truewit center of manners comedy, the portrayal of appropriate social behavior set in opposition to hollow aping, as we saw in chapter four, or to a total inability or unwillingness to share in society's highest aspirations, failings highlighted in the present section.

To conclude, we have noted that the outsider figure takes several forms in Molière and finds richer comic expression than in Restoration comedy. Whether single-minded boors, self-blinded monomaniacs, ambitious burghers, libidinous prudes, or alien professionals, Molière gives ample scope to those who stand in opposition to the values enshrined by *le beau monde*. But the real outsiders on both sides of the Channel are the overwhelming majority of the population—peasants and city-dwellers—totally excluded from representation in manners comedy, even as foils. A narrow urban elite set the tone in both Paris and London; their elevated banter was alone worthy of emulation, and even the middle class, when it appeared in caricatured form, was shown to be a comfortable *bourgeoisie* living in comparative luxury. The lower strata were material only for the earthiest comic treatment, and playwrights who gave in to the temptations of low farce were likely to be reminded, as was Molière by a custodian of taste like Boileau, that their aim should be loftier: "Etudiez la Cour et connaissez la Ville."

CONCLUSION

The purpose of the foregoing has been to interpret Molière's theater in the light of criteria traditionally associated with Restoration manners comedy. We have thus endeavored to validate the underlying assumption that a considerable number of Molière plays can be thought of as specimens of "genteel" comedy akin to that of the Restoration, a comedy reflecting, like its English counterpart, the social values of an upper-class elite. This approach to Molière has carried with it, of course, a comparison with Restoration drama. The analysis of common traits has shown, I hope, that the two comic traditions share much more than hitherto had been assumed. Earlier comparisons foundered ultimately on debatable questions of influence arising from overblown historical links. Even attempts to see the two as roughly contemporaneous but distinct manifestations of the comic spirit yielded little of interest in the past, similarities were dwarfed by the supposed chasm separating the two comic productions in terms of stagecraft, dramatic structure, and *Weltanschauung*. However, a half-century after the last thoroughgoing study of Molière and Restoration comedy, we are now able to profit from recent directions in Molière scholarship to propose a new, vital relationship between the two most enduring manifestations of comedy in seventeenth-century Europe.

It is time now to summarize the argument developed in the foregoing pages and to ponder its implication in terms of sociocritical criteria. What in comedy may appear to us as a distortion of reality, an idealizing or satirical perspective on facets of the time, reveals in fact a more subtle and meaningful reality: the values, tastes, ideological assumptions to which art gives its own form and its own outlook. After reviewing the resemblances and divergences between Molière and Restoration comedy, I will examine some of the more striking ways in which, on both sides of the Channel, the species of comedy just analyzed ignored, even falsified, historical fact in order to celebrate more freely and imaginatively the aspirations to which lived reality gives rise.

As we saw in chapter two, Restoration manners comedy owes its dynamics to the interaction of three groups of characters: truewits, witwouds, and the witless, as they are usually labeled. The analysis of similar types in Molière, with appropriate parallels from across the Channel, was the business of the subsequent chapters. I stressed costume-coding in particular as a key to typology. From the very first appearance, a character's most visible and most easily decoded sign—dress—alerts the audience as to appropriate reactions and expectations. The gallants among the truewits respect prevailing fashions, but with taste and discretion. Their elegant uniform—*justaucorps*, *haut-de-chausses*, wig, *jabot*, brightly decorated hat, and decorously unaccented sword—bear witness to their rank and social status. In all the plays I have analyzed, there is at least one lover to provide a focal point of vestimentary norms for the play, and, with surprising frequency, he is pictured by Brissart. Standard effects of contrast reinforce his perceived exemplariness. Although fops occur with relative rarity in Molière, when they do appear it is with indices of fashion exaggerated to the point that they seem absurd affectations. These lackwits generally embody such jollity, however, that we tend to laugh *with* them as well at *at* them. The outsider group, on the other hand, display by their costume a total disharmony with the young blades. The *pourpoint*, cloak, plain hat (either the wide-brimmed *bourgeois* one or the floppy beret of the clown tradition), and particularly the absence of two signs, the wig and the sword, denote their social mediocrity and incompatibility with genteel behavior. In the Brissart illustrations, for example, we see either a Sganarelle-type uniform vaguely reminiscent of the *commedia dell'arte* or the sober black clothing worn by Orgon and Harpagon. Often these costumes are made to seem quaintly out-of-date, as with the ruff sported by several Sganarelles or Harpagon.

It is no accident that Chauveau and Brissart often chose, as their freeze-frame emblem of the whole play, a moment when gallant and outsider meet, so that the discordance of the latter can be the more forcefully marked. Sometimes a trick perpetrated against the outsider is suggested as well, as when Valère kisses Isabelle's hand behind an unaware Sganarelle (*L'Ecole des maris*, no. 6) or when the disguised painter in *Le Sicilien* courts his lady literally behind Don Pèdre's back (no. 16). We remember too that actors were not alone on stage; on many occasions in Molière's day, more than thirty spectators sat on either side of the playing area. In general they were young men dressed in the latest fashion. Although some may have been foolishly ostentatious, it would be wrong to think of them as a clutch of preening fops. Eraste, the truewit of *Les Fâcheux*, obviously thought it perfectly normal to take his place "sur le théâtre" and deplored only the fact that his theatergoing *fâcheux* sat in front of the players, not in the proper area on the side. As theater historians like Herzel have observed, the rest of the audience must have associated the stage spectator with the play and its costuming. The presence of a lover, dressed with the same tasteful elegance as the gentlemen seated on stage, must have established a visual—and by implication, social—bond between the truewit character and the truewit spectator. Noting the example of *L'Ecole des maris*, Herzel points out that Valère's "suitability is immediately ratified by the visual harmony between him and the members of the audience who serve as frame to the stage picture" ("The Decor of Molière's Stage," p. 928).

This observation puts the question of stage spectators in a rather more positive light than is usually the case. Conventional wisdom on the subject speaks of a maddening custom tolerated only because of the income it provided. Though every *sou* no doubt counted to maintain an ever-precarious solvency, it is easy to exaggerate the revenue from the onstage audience. During the 1672–73 season at the Palais-Royal, a rather good one if we are to judge from La Grange's *Registre*, the average number of stage spectators per performance was ten, with extremes of none at all to thirty-six. Of the total audience, they represented about four percent, and they provided only nine percent of box-office receipts.[1] At that time spectators could have been removed from the stage without a major financial dislocation; boxes for the same type of audience existed for exactly the same price. Later in the century, when the stage audience at the d'Orbay Comédie-Française could number well over one hundred, its revenue became no doubt crucial. In any event, public visibility was highly prized as an important way of validating one's claim to distinction, and no doubt some theatergoers found great self-gratification in being on stage. And it could very well have been a symbiotic relationship, with spectators used as visual signs by the playwright to channel audience reaction in general and thus to highlight social relevance.

After 1690 spectators were to be found on the Restoration stage too, and they must have had a similar framing role for an action that in both capitals took place well downstage. The brief examination in chapter one of the playhouse in Paris and London revealed some striking parallels in audience composition and distribution, in the function of scenic design, and especially in the playing area and its relationship with the audience. To appreciate the staging of Molière's plays and Restoration comedy, we must make a conscious effort to rid ourselves of what we have learned to expect from the modern realistic theater. No rigid conceptual line separated actor from audience. The playing space was in front of the proscenium arch or under it, in an area often encompassed visually by the hall itself; on both sides of the Channel, the line of side balconies could extend over the apron, so that the playing space could be perceived as jutting into the audience's spatial purview. The convention of downstage acting placed the player very close not only to the stage spectators but to those in the close boxes and in the pit as well. It is not difficult to imagine a resulting sense of complicity and unspoken interaction, further enhanced by relatively continuous lighting—the audience was not in the modern-day dark of collective anonymity—and the uninhibited conduct, related no doubt to their visibility, of spectators all too eager to cheer and jeer. In all this the scenery, which for us in the modern realistic drama encompasses and defines the character, could serve only as an emblematic marker, a merely schematic indication of locale, however realistic it strove to be. Indeed, the doctrinaire illusionism of l'abbé d'Aubignac, for example, for whom there had to be a rigid separation of story and spectacle, of "histoire" and "représentation" (*Pratique*, p. 45), was in fact constantly undermined by theater practice. The only real concession to such theorizing was the convention by which the player kept his persona for the whole play, so that there was rarely any confusion between himself in his actor's identity and the role he was assuming; a corollary of this rule was that the presence of the audience was hardly ever acknowledged in the text itself, although such devices as the monologue and the aside allowed the actor to play to the spectator without openly breaching the gap between them.

However important theatrical actualization may be, it still must arise from a text, an order of words supported by a value structure that gives it immediate relevance. Molière and Restoration comedy reflected a many-faceted ideal of social practice that we have conveniently summarized under one general heading, "wit," *esprit*. We observed that the Restoration comedy of "wit" implies, beyond a surface aptitude for verbal inventiveness and *à propos*, a celebration of the whole of social exemplarity with its most prized ingredients of tact, judgment, and natural grace. We have seen that in Molière much the same notions are suggested by *esprit* in the wide meaning of "l'esprit du monde," a phrase denoting something not unlike *honnêteté*, that wide-ranging concept of social propriety linked to upper-class behavior without being the exclusive purview of the noble orders. The *honnêtes gens* are above all social assets; definitions invariably revolve around the basic idea of pleasurable company, as in Méré's famous phrase: "L'honnêteté . . . ce n'est autre chose que d'exceller en tout ce qui regarde les agréments et les bienséances de la vie."[2] Here the chief component elements find concise expression: striving for distinction, ability to entertain, and awareness of propriety.

In terms of dramatic impact, the weight of example is often negative in Molière; the "heavy father" plays depend on the satire of inappropriate conduct, the ridicule attendant upon breaches in the social code. Thus Arnolphe, Orgon, Harpagon demonstrate proper social practice in a negative way, by implication. But it would be wrong, as I have argued, to discount the positive illustrations of "l'esprit du monde" in Molière's theater. Not only do the recurrent truewit uniform of the young gallant and the fashionable dress worn by his lady convey visually the presence of vestimentary norms, but in most of Molière's manners plays we also find characters who, in word and deed as well, proffer a strong image of exemplarity. The categorization and description of such personages was the business of chapter three. The truewits of *La Critique de l'Ecole des femmes*, for example, ensure bright, witty conversation and have enough mastery over themselves to remain this side of acrimony. Eraste in *Les Fâcheux* shows courtliness toward his beloved and a certain forbearance to the crowd of importunate people he must confront. Molière makes us think of Restoration truewits in this manner, as well as in a strain of cynicism where deceit and victim-baiting are put in a positive light. The humiliations suffered by George Dandin, Monsieur de Pourceaugnac, and La Comtesse d'Escarbagnas, the bilking of which Monsieur Jourdain is a victim, are perceived as deserved; and the truewits go about their deceiving ways with impunity—indeed, with contentment—at the play's end: Clitandre will cuckold Dandin with Angélique's connivance, a wedding will reward Pourceaugnac's tormentors, Julie and the sneering Vicomte will marry, and Dorante and Dorimène plight their troth in Jourdain's treasure-house.

Thus, in the final analysis, the way of the world takes precedence, and high principles of integrity and plain-dealing evaporate in the jungle of human relationships. As a matter of fact, one of the problems we encountered in discussing positive behavior was the articulation between social norms and morality. *Honnêteté* often pays only lip service to abstract virtue. Furetière makes it but an afterthought in defining *l'honnête homme* as "qui a pris l'air du monde, qui sait vivre, qui a du mérite et de la probité."[3] The difficulty, obviously, is that moral principles may conflict with social practice. Truth-telling can be admired in the abstract, but its effects on social *agrément* could be, as *Le Misanthrope* so eloquently demonstrates, devastating. The cause for this state of affairs was perceived, naturally, as human vanity, the self-blindness and self-preoccupation that prevents us from acknowledging our shortcomings. We thus rejoin a comic form of the great seventeenth-century meditations on *amour-propre* that reached their most urbane expression in La Rochefoucauld's *Maximes*. In such a world of warring egoisms, virtue must be either a sham or a dangerous vulnerability; the preferable and safer quality was lucidity about the way of the world and a cultivation of the kind of behavior necessary to survive in society and make the company of one's fellow human beings as pleasant as possible.

This sense of the hollowness of conventional morality and the law of the jungle underlying the refinements of *le bel air* was especially acute in the Restoration. The cynicism and amorality of the rake, the opportunism and hypocrisy of the libidinous coquette, even the calculating, free-speaking manner of the polite gentlewoman, so offensive to those who would like to affirm the goodness of man, are all responses to this essential pessimism. To quote from Peter Holland's penetrating analysis: "Restoration comedy posits . . . a society that, in its warm humanity, is essentially corrupt and impure; it allows for the existence of evil. The presentation of virtue must be either a product of total control over the methods of that society [Mirabell], or a hollow, supra-social ideal figure [Fidelia] (and also the sentimental heroine)" (p. 57).

That Molière's theater "allows for the existence of evil" is incontestable; if things go badly in his plays, it is because of human vanity and abuse of power. But no comedy can confine itself to a consistent portrait of unregenerate vice. The genre must carry some seed of hope and optimism if it is to present the image of a society that is a collective aspiration. Thus there was in Restoration comedy an embodiment of relative virtue presented from within, in a character who, like Mirabell, can manipulate a corrupt world to desirable ends; or playwrights resorted to an implausible solution springing from beyond the given elements in the play. Thus Fidelia manages to survive, chaste and idealistic, and not only win her man but persuade him that there is good in mankind.[4] We find both solutions in Molière. Ariste in *Les Femmes savantes* manages to right the situation from within by adroitly exposing Trissotin's cynical greed. More characteristically, however, Molière resorts to the comic miracle. Instead of a principle of virtue within the play, he presents a *deus ex machina* in varied forms but which all presuppose some kind of providential force—royal or otherwise—capable of mastering the evil tendencies in man. And more than in the Restoration, Molière contrasts his portrayal of vice with guilelessness and sentimentality in his young heroes and heroines.

From a manners standpoint, then, many parallels between Molière and Restoration comedy come to the fore. But it is possible to structure the depiction of manners in many different ways, and in such areas as plot development, dialogue, and overall tone we are aware of the fundamental differences. Restoration comedy continues a tradition of dramaturgy that harks back to the beginning of English theater. The action moves from one scene, one locale, to another, a technique that affords a panoramic view of the society depicted and allows for a multiplicity of subplots. Even within a given scene—a public thoroughfare, for instance—considerable numbers of characters may come and go. By this processional technique, Restoration comedy conveys an improvisational, spontaneous impression that adds greatly to its charm, and the shifting venues allow for a wide sampling of society.

This *intrigue à tiroirs* is not foreign to Molière's theater, as the example of *Les Fâcheux* has shown. Here a fashionable gathering place and the chance encounters it encourages lead to a panoramic impression. As with Restoration comedy in general, Molière's *Les Fâcheux* seems structured to produce an amusing, ever-new gallery of social types. The traditional "maisons et rues" decor that prevails in his early plays also encourages the chance comings and goings that characterize comedy across the Channel. But when Molière shifts his setting to the confines of a private house, character interaction has to be more explicitly motivated; the relative isolation and privacy of family life preclude unexpected, spontaneous intrusion by outsiders. As a result the depiction of society becomes perforce narrower.

Molière's fixed settings, then, inhibit the kind of freewheeling structure typical of Restoration comedies. Even more significantly, the convention of the *liaison de scènes* dampens any impulse to multiple-thread development. During an act the stage is never left empty, the temporal continuity never broken. Scene divisions mark arrivals and departures, but one or more personages are on stage to ensure a direct link to what precedes and follows. In contrast the freedom to bring an entirely new set of characters on stage during an act, in a different place and possibly at a different time, accounts in part at least for the tendency in Restoration comedy to complex, multilevel plots.

So far we have not considered what is customarily thought of as the chief difference between Molière and Restoration comedy—respect for, and disregard of, the unities. The importance of the so-called rules has been considerably exaggerated. Molière never adhered to them slavishly, and indeed they were never applied in all their rigor to comedy. To consider unity of place, always defined rather generally: not only in *Dom Juan* with its multiple locales but in such "regular" comedies as *L'Avare* and *Le Malade imaginaire*, Molière wrote setting changes into his plays. Unity of time, or "La règle des vingt-quatre heures," was more specific, but did not preclude the *structure à tiroirs*, as Congreve himself showed when he adhered with apparent effortlessness to this unity in *The Way of the World*: "The time equal to that of the presentation," he asserts, with some exaggeration, in the *Dramatis Personae*. As for unity of action, the underlying intent was to discourage the gratuitous and unmotivated; it was sufficient, however, to prepare in some vague way a later, normally implausible development. Thus in *L'Avare* the romantic circumstances of Valère's meeting with Elise before the play begins, and the riddle of Valère's own birth, added to the mystery of Mariane's origin are sufficient to make the final reversal conform more or less to unity of action. Moreover, a bewilderingly complex action did not necessarily violate this unity, as some of Corneille's later tragedies make abundantly clear (*Héraclius*, for example).

Molière did in fact favor a fairly simple plot, centering on a single conflict between generations, between factions in a household, between young love and old tyranny. This concentration is rare in Restoration comedy; but in fairness to the latter, what Molière gains in density and cohesion, he loses in scope. We behold a wider, more detailed picture of the whole of Restoration society, as opposed to Molière's more confined image. The closed world of *Le Misanthrope* explodes with *The Plain-Dealer* into a vast, satiric panorama of sailors, lawyers, fops, coquettes, in their various settings.

Salient differences in dialogue and tone must also be noted. Molière's carefully wrought verse texts like that of *Tartuffe* or *Le Misanthrope*, with their respect for the set piece and stylized, symmetrical speeches, stand in contrast to the more natural, flowing prose dialogue of Restoration comedy. We find little in Molière of the characteristic epigrammatic banter of Restoration comedy: a more satiric voice obtrudes, running the gamut from light irony to confrontational vehemence. The free-and-easy cynicism of the Restoration reflects as well a less demanding standard of behavior. It is obvious that gentlemen and gentlewomen in English comedy were allowed a much greater range of expression and conduct than in the French plays. Roguish antics were tolerated, even applauded in the gallants, and young women enjoyed a social freedom that in Molière was afforded only young widows like Célimène or the Dorimène of *Le Bourgeois gentilhomme*. The machinations and hypocrisy of the lustful Restoration coquette were given much wider portraiture too than Molière's discreet presentation of the type. A characteristic refusal to take anything seriously, particularly marriage, constitutes too a major difference with Molière. His romantic side, nurtured in the earnest, stylized language of the Italian *innamorati* and influenced by the pastoral-type comedy of earlier decades, tended to picture mutually acceptable marriage in fairy-story rosiness.

Molière's relative seriousness, the greater dramatic concentration of his plays, and his more deliberate craftsmanship have tempted the comparative scholar to find a kindred spirit in the great classicist of English drama, Ben Jonson. We would do well to reconsider the *rapprochement*, since it is a key point, alleged or implied, by those who would see little in common between Molière and Restoration comedy. The dispersed dramatic interest of the latter, its extensive gallery of personages, seem indeed to stand in contrast to Jonson's insular world with a powerfully drawn character at the center, a world similar, it has been held, to Molière's. In short, Molière and Jonson both pass as "humor" dramatists.

An impartial scanning of Jonson's theater uncovers obvious differences from the start. On the level of dramaturgy, Jonson belongs squarely in the great English tradition of multilinear development consonant with an action that moves freely from one locale to another—the characteristic dramatic mode, as we have noted, of Restoration comedy. More importantly, Jonson's portrayal of eccentricity is very different from Molière's. Take Morose, the chief character of *The Silent Woman*, a play often likened to Molière's monomaniacal comedies like *L'Avare*. Morose hates noise, a revulsion not uncommon in his world—or ours. But this personage is the victim of a bizarre, exaggerated humor that triggers hostile reactions at the slightest sound, even the human voice. Jonson's imagination runs wild in depicting the various grotesque indices of this single-minded preoccupation. The anecdotes told about him remind us of the comic revelations concerning Harpagon's obsessional conduct; but Molière's miser alludes in his actions to a whole social ethos of which he is an embodied antithesis. On the contrary, the implied message of Morose's *idée fixe* seems merely that we must accept noise as a part of living. Molière's attention to social signs, to the observed reality that he converts into comic substance, conjures up the image of a recognizable world, that of the Paris *bourgeoisie* bearing the stigma of vestigial mercantile instincts. With Jonson we are absorbed into a claustrophobic, oppressive setting cut off from normal society, a trait especially evident in his better-known works *Volpone* and *The Alchemist*. What strikes us there is the extreme force of the ruling passion and its preposterous manifestations. Yet even in dramas with an open, contemporary setting like *The Silent Woman*, *Every Man in his Humour*, or *Bartholomew Fair*, Jonson conjures up from his powerful imagination a personal, idiosyncratic world that seems his distinctive mark.

We must not forget either that Molière's monomaniacs stand in opposition to a romantic *élan* that usually defeats them. The gallant and his lady are pervasive enough to carry a normative function. On the other hand, sentimentality is virtually nonexistent in Jonson. The courting male is seldom seen in action, even in a play like *Every Man in his Humour*, where Edward Knowell ends up marrying Mrs. Bridget. Finally, Jonson's rather self-conscious humanism, his pride in the classical lore he has scrupulously assimilated, make him a creature rather different from Molière, a worldly man of the theater for whom learned display would violate the very *urbanité* at the center of his social vision. All things considered, Molière is more Congreve's brother than a son of Ben.

I have tried in the foregoing chapters to grasp in some measure the *Weltanschauung* implicit in Molière's theater and in Restoration comedy. The plays themselves have been the chief documentary material. I have emphasized that drama, like any form of writing, offers only an interpretation of the realities of a time. Even "objective" accounts—letters, annals, histories—must show the biases of their authors. Much more, then, must we be attentive to the way in which comedy twists and schematizes the data drawn from observation. A comedy of manners obeys two laws, one relating to the veracity of its portrayal of social reality (a portrayal itself subject to distortion), the other governed by generic imperatives, what comedy as a form imposes. Thus if Arnolphe has "arrived," we might expect him to wear the fashionable dress of a former *bourgeois* living nobly, and such indeed is his costume in recent period interpretations of the play. But convention dictates that the gallant, repeatedly pictured by Brissart as a fashionable young blade, be set in contrast with the *barbon*'s world: unfashionable, archaic, dissonant. Thus Arnolphe, as well as Harpagon, Mariane's ludicrous suitor, must exemplify a certain dress code in contrast to that of the genuine *amoureux*.

Comic representation, then, is one thing; historical reality is another. What indeed *was* the social fact, and how was it transposed by comic convention? I have already spoken of the great masses of common folk—peasants, urban workers, shopkeepers—who, though comprising the overwhelming majority of the population in both countries, found only sparse, sneering representation in manners comedy. In each realm there was a reigning elite—the old *gentilhommerie* coupled with a growing intermediate class (the recently ennobled and the gentry in England, the *noblesse de robe* in France). This more diffuse aristocracy was augmented by more and more members of the mercantile castes who bought ennobling offices in their thirst for social advancement. This composite elite was spread throughout the whole country, since there were powerful urban centers in the provinces, prosperous and culturally alive. But the comedy of manners, we have had ample occasion to observe, downgraded everything, no matter how intrinsically lofty, that was not Paris or London. A first, major distortion of historical fact, then: only the capital counts in the representation of a country's mores.

The capital, of course, belonged to the king and basked in his light. It was to his interest to overvalue Paris, or London, for his subjects were drawn increasingly from the provinces, where they could be fractious, to the capital, where they could be observed and subjected to the rule of etiquette. For besides political power, the monarch exercised an indirect social control through cultural imperatives. Thus *honnêteté* must be seen as something more than a laudable aspiration to excellence and civility; it was a means to social, and thus political, domination. Albanese pinpoints accurately this hegemonic function:

> On voit à quel point les "bonnes mannières" issues de la doctrine de l'honnêteté prennent une fonction régulatrice. C'est qu'elles servent à rendre anonymes les honnêtes gens, à les neutraliser en quelque sorte si bien que l'honnête homme, inhibé par le tabou social, ne critique pas. Réduits à une espèce d'uniformité collective, les nobles et les bourgeois "honnêtes" mènent côte à côte, une existence strictement régie par les impératifs de la cérémonie rituelle qu'impose la société honnête. (*Le Dynamisme de la peur*, p. 36)

With the decay of the ancient nobility, its ideal of the *gentilhomme* with its concomitant notion of lofty independence was being replaced by the homogenizing ethic of the less class-distinct *honnête homme*, where individualism was confined to an art of worldly living within the limits of a tight social orthodoxy.

Not only did the code of *honnêteté* enhance the king's authority over his high-ranking and potentially rebellious subjects, but it legitimized as well the domination that the whole elite—Court and Town—exercised over the masses below. As Stanton points out, we have here a "conspicuous leisure" aristocracy in Veblen's terms, dedicated to the cultivation, to quote Stanton's paraphrase, "of nonutilitarian skills and the systematic refinement of a personal worldly manner, not only from the sense of the indignity of productive work, but also from a desire to display a capacity for idleness in such immaterial form as 'manners and breeding, polite usage, decorum.'. . . These accomplishments, which cannot be attained by those who have to work, become 'vouchers' of a life of leisure. The time, strenuous application and discipline which they require constitute the only 'labor' deemed worthy of an aristo- crat" (*The Aristocrat as Art*, p. 2). Thus the upper classes justified their golden idleness and their right to profit from the labors of their inferiors.

The very vagueness of terms like *les honnêtes gens*, the upper classes, betokens a society where the old, rigid orders have been eroded and the traditional distinctions blurred, primarily by an *arriviste* mercantile class eager for status. The landed aristocracy in England was beginning to lose its hold, and a moneyed Whig elite, more attentive to trade and industry, was on the rise. The same held true in France with bankers, financiers, traders, speculators amassing considerable fortunes while the great noble families often fell into hardship. Curiously enough, though Molière showed only one moneylender in his theater, wealthy Frenchmen of all ranks made a habit of lending vast sums to the state, the *emprunt* being, along with the standard taxes and the sale of more and more offices, the chief means of capital accumulation for Louis XIV's grandiose projects and costly wars. Another reality cen- sored by manners comedy: such trafficking is shown unworthy of men of distinction; only a knavish *bourgeois* could sink so low.

In reality the newly rich burgher class did enjoy a limited up- ward mobility. Ultimately it was the king who encouraged this accession and who regulated it by imposing certain steps and procedures. The "first noblemen of their lineage," as La Bruyère so bitterly labeled them,[5] were thus royal creatures, living in a symbiotic relationship with the sovereign; his coffers gained in weight, and they gained the right to erase their humble past and validate their present claims. The essential was to live nobly, to rub off all lower-class taints, to hide behind the facade of upper- class bearing. Consequently, distinctions in Molière between "bourgeois" plays like *Tartuffe*, *L'Avare*, or *Les Femmes savantes* and "aristocratic" comedies like *Le Misanthrope*, though perhaps useful as overall categories, are of limited value in delimiting social attitudes. In many plays—*bourgeois* or otherwise—there is a gallant invariably pictured as a young aristocrat, sword at side. Brissart shows Philinte dressed no differently from Valère in *L'Avare* or Eraste in *L'Ecole des maris*. The decor of *Tartuffe* represents an interior no less sumptuous than that of *Le Misanthrope*. Although not in noble attire, Arnolphe and Orgon possess the essential status symbol, land, and obviously derive income from it. If they cannot be shown visibly as aristocrats, it is because, as I have contended, the polarities of comedy demand a contrast between generations and an appropriate outward coding of that contrast. Their appearance as burghers denotes, moreover, an inward character. They must be signaled as mired in the meanest traits of their class of birth—tyranny and pettiness—and thus insensitive to the subtleties of aristocratic social procedure.

Two features stand out in this comic rendering of social reality. The first is the compelling perspective from on high. It is through the eyes of "la Cour et la Ville," the snobbish Town centers, that we view the rest of society. As has been evident all through this study, a powerful insider-outsider dialectic isolates the happy few from the teeming masses. Those living beyond the capital are condemned to the tedium to which their coarseness reduces them. Provincials in both France and England are held in contempt, being at best foolish pretenders to metropolitan fashion. Within the capital ordinary people are relegated to the outer edges; when they appear episodically, in the guise of servants or, in England, orange-women and the like, it is as inferior beings often treated with contempt or patronizing solicitude. The mercantile classes, the "citizen" in London, the *bon bourgeois* of the French capital are all derided as acquisitive, jealous, mean-spirited; from their ranks are drawn the cuckolds of comedy, Arnolphe and Pinchwife. Even among the titled, fops and coxcombs draw our laughter for their affected and exaggerated behavior. Thus, by a process of comic elimination, we return to the top, the truewits of English comedy, Molière's *honnêtes gens* conversant with "l'esprit du monde."

There is ample evidence that the theater audience, though dominated, if not in numbers at least in presiding values, by the aristocracy, was a reasonably mixed one, with burghers as frequent attenders. How then did this multifaceted audience not only accept a social vision as narrow and smug as the one just summarized but suffer some of its component elements to be derided by that very elite? How could a citizen, a *bourgeois*, be party to the continual sniping that was his fate in Restoration comedy and in Molière's theater? One can only offer some conjectures. To begin with, the question implies a class consciousness that is perhaps anachronistic when applied to the seventeenth century. The prestige and authority at the top was not contested in the name of competing sociopolitical philosophies. A burgher eager to spend a fortune accumulated over many years to buy an ennobling title or office is proof enough that no other organization of society was imagined at the time. Also, theatergoers of any era have considerable powers of dissociation that comic caricature, particularly, makes readily operative. A stage satire of a psychiatrist would not necessarily upset a practitioner in the audience, no more than a farmer would take offense at the depiction of a bumbling, ill-spoken hayseed. A real miser in Molière's audience would probably have described himself self-servingly as a man of thrift, at the furthest remove from the grasping inhumanity of a Harpagon. The abject fools in Molière eager for social advancement were probably mocked unabashedly by the very spectators who had themselves recently scurried to buy titles and other appurtenances of status.

The second point relates to the conservative image of society reflected in the comedy we have been analyzing. Each estate is portrayed in a feudal stasis, fixed forever in its proper place in the social hierarchy. Those who would ascend the social scale are doomed to ridicule. The accent is thus on the ceiling above each stratum that resists any effort to penetrate it. Justifying this image of fixity is the belief, a profoundly ideological one useful for social order and stability, that the proper conduct needed for acceptance among the elite cannot be learned. It is given as a natural grace to the wellborn, and those who would have it taught betray quickly their basic and irremediable inferiority. All this is amply illustrated by the bumpkin, the citizen in Restoration comedy and such characters as Monsieur Jourdain and George Dandin in Molière. In a word, only the elite truly merit the good life. It is no coincidence that Molière's satires of illegitimate social climbing were staged principally for the Court.

On the other hand, the mechanisms of social advancement historically present and very operative—even if they were generally scorned—are only scantily depicted in comedy. Instead of showing how higher status could be obtained—marriage into the noble orders, acquisition of land, purchase of titles and offices—comedy presents the counterforce of closure as all-powerful. Thus we find yet once more in comedy a major distortion of historical realities. Again possible explanations may be advanced. For a start, comedy may be held to be conservative by its very nature. It celebrates order both by the negative picture of disruption it shows and the return to harmony and permanence that its dénouement habitually signifies—a re-turn, indeed, a recovery of something existing earlier.[6] Apart from any golden-age connotations, however, comedy enshrines a kind of providentialism, an image of stability reassuring in any age but especially for the one that frames this study. The seventeenth century in both England and France was poised on the threshold of major changes. But though the threat to perennial values was dimly felt, no new social concepts had emerged to validate and encompass what was to come. The bourgeois on the rise had no real sense yet of their own identity. They could affirm their importance only by the indices of a class into which they were not born, by the cultivation of an aristocratic life style, an upper-class ethos that included, paradoxically, the belief in rigid, immutable class distinctions.

A final point may be made concerning this dominant image of closure in a relatively open society. If social ascension is to be meaningful, it must be made to seem rare. If the happy few are shown as submerged by the aspiring many, the resulting image would devalue the very purpose of social climbing. To quote a witticism from Gilbert and Sullivan, "When everyone is somebodee, then no one's anybody!"[7] Consequently there must be a myth of non-accessibility prohibiting advancement to all but a select coterie and justified by the tenet of inborn excellence. Thus the weight of closure in comedy, the opprobrium heaped upon usurpation, constituted an imaginative means by which social advancement could be validated as a rare event within an apparently stable social structure. It may well be that on both sides of the Channel comedy provided some measure of reassurance and justification for a society apprehensively in transition, nostalgic for fading social verities and clinging tenuously to an eroding here-and-now.

APPENDIX

P. Brissart, d.   I. Sauvé, F.

LES CONTRETEMPS

Figure 1

P.Brissart d. I.Sauvé F.

LE DEPIT AMOUREUX

Figure 2

LES PRECIEUSES RIDICULES

Figure 3

P. Brissart d.   J. Sauvé f.

LE COCU IMAGINAIRE

Figure 4

Figure 5

L'ESCOLE DES MARIS

Figure 6

P. Brissart d. J. Sauue f.

LES FACHEUX

Figure 7

L'ESCOLE DES FEMMES

Figure 8

I. Sauué fec.

LA CRITIQ. DE LESCOLE DES FÉMES

Figure 9

IMPROMPTV DE VERSAILLE

Figure 10

P. Brissart d.   I. Sauué f.

LE MARIAGE FORCÉ

Figure 11

L'AMOUR MEDECIN

Figure 12

Figure 13

Brisart d.   I Sauué F

LE MISANTROPE

Figure 14

Figure 15

P. Brisart d.   I Sauvé f.

L'AMOVR PEINTRE

Figure 16

GEORGE DANDIN

Figure 17

L'AVARE

Figure 18

LE TARTVFFE

Figure 19

Brisart d.   J. Sauve f.

L'Imposteur

Figure 20

M. DE POURCEAUGNAC

Figure 21

P. Brisart d.

I. Sauvé f.

LA COMTESSE DE SCARMAGNAS

Figure 22

P. Brissart d.

J. Sauvé f.

LES FEMMES SCAVANTES

Figure 23

Brifart d.   Sonne f.

LE MALADE IMAGINAIRE

Figure 24

NOTES

INTRODUCTION

1.   John Wilcox, *The Relation of Molière to Restoration Comedy* (New York, 1938).

2.   Wilcox provides a good summary of the influence debate and its nationalistic undercurrents (pp. 1–17). The tradition of source quantification goes back to Langbaine's *An Account of English Dramatic Poets* of 1691. An extreme nineteenth-century example is Henri Van Laun's significantly titled "Les Plagiaires de Molière en Angleterre," published in *Le Moliériste* 2 (1880–81) and 3 (1881–82). The contrary opinion was vigorously promoted by John Palmer in his pioneering book *The Comedy of Manners* (London, 1913), one of the first studies to free Restoration comedy from the strictures of Victorian morality and to stress its uniqueness—even to the point of exaggeration: "Restoration comedy owed almost as little to France as to the English school it displaced [the Jonsonian comedy of humours]" (p. 66).

3.   "Sir George Etherge. A Neglected Chapter of English Literature," *Cornhill Magazine*, 43 (1881): 284–304.

4.   Dudley Miles, *The Influence of Molière on Restoration Comedy* (New York, 1910). Miles's book was republished in pocket format by Octagon books in 1971 and thus remains a strong presence, no matter how outdated its methdology and thesis.

5.   Bonamy Dobrée, *Restoration Comedy 1660–1720* (Oxford, 1924). This book remains an engaging and informative one.

6.   Thomas Fujimura, *The Restoration Comedy of Wit* (Princeton, N.J., 1952).

7.   Kenneth Muir, *The Comedy of Manners* (London, 1970), p. 11.

8.   David Hirst, *The Comedy of Manners* (London, 1979), pp. 14–16.

9.   Norman Holland, *The First Modern Comedies* (Cambridge, Mass., 1959), p. 206.

10.   A few scattered articles have appeared, e.g.: Hilary Semple, "Molière

and Restoration Comedy," *English Studies in Africa* 18 (1975): 71–84; N. Suckling, "Molière and English Restoration Comedy," *Restoration Theatre*, ed. J. R. Brown and B. Harris, Stratford-Upon-Avon Studies 6 (1965): 93–107. Studies of wider scope are few and far between. André de Mandach's *Molière et la comédie de moeurs en Angleterre 1660–1668* (Neuchâtel, 1946) is much more narrowly focused than its title would indicate. Mandach's rather unconvincing thesis is that *Sir Martin Marall*, an adaptation of *L'Etourdi* usually attributed to Dryden, was in fact penned by the duke of Newcastle.

11.   Peter Holland, *The Ornament of Action: Text and Performance in Restoration Comedy* (Cambridge, 1979), p. 58.

12.   *Le Registre de La Grange 1659–1685*, ed. B. E. Young and G. P. Young (Paris, 1947), 1:145.

13.   See *The London Stage* (Carbondale, Ill., 1960–), passim.

14.   The figure is based on the plays labeled "comedy" in Allardyce Nicoll's hand-list printed at the end of his *A History of Restoration Drama 1660–1700* (Cambridge, 1923), pp. 348–76.

15.   Ashley Thorndyke, *English Comedy* (New York, 1929), p. 341.

16.   Kathleen Lynch, in her influential *The Restoration Mode of Comedy* (Ann Arbor, Mich., 1927), analyzes these antecedents in some detail (pp. 11–42).

17.   For manners traits in Corneille, see my "Corneille and the Comedy of Manners," *PFSCL* 11 (1984): 393–407.

18.   L. C. Knights, "Restoration Comedy: The Reality and the Myth," in *Explorations* (London, 1946), p. 149.

19.   Will G. Moore, *Molière: A New Criticism* (Oxford, 1949).

20.   René Bray, *Molière homme de théâtre* (Paris, 1954).

21.   Paul Bénichou, *Morales du grand siècle* (Paris, 1948), pp. 156–218.

22.   For a remarkably evenhanded and comprehensive *état présent* of the various trends in Molière scholarship, see Marie-Odile Sweetser, "Situation de la recherche: domaines de la critique moliéresque," *Oeuvres et critiques* 6 (1981): 9–28.

23.   The following titles are of special note: J. Brody, "*Dom Juan* and *Le Misanthrope*, or the Esthetics of Individualism in Molière," *PMLA* 84 (1969): 559–76, and "Esthétique et société chez Molière, in *Dramaturgie et société*, ed. J. Jacquot (Paris, 1968), 1:307–26; W. D. Howarth, *Molière: A Playwright and His Audience* (Cambridge, 1982); F. Lawrence, "*Tartuffe*: A Question of *Honnête* behavior," *RN* 15 (1974): 134–44; J. Mesnard, "*Le Misanthrope*, mise en question de l'art de plaire," *RHLF* 72 (1972): 853–89; J. Morel, "Molière ou la dramaturgie de l'honnêteté," *Information Littéraire* 15 (1963): 185–91. Recent books concerned more generally with social norms implicit in *honnêteté* also have relevance to Molière: J. P. Dens, *L'Honnête homme et la critique de goût: esthétique et société au XVIIe siècle* (Lexington, Ky., 1981); D. Stanton, *The Aristocrat as Art* (New York, 1980). Finally, my *Molière: An Archetypal Approach* (Toronto, 1976), while stressing general

comic patterns, endeavors to relate them as much as possible to the historical and social realities of Molière's time. The present study constitutes a more rigorous application of sociocritical methodology, with Restoration comedy as a point of comparison.

24.   Two Molière scholars have come to the forefront: Ralph Albanese, Jr., *Le Dynamisme de la peur chez Molière* (University, Miss., 1976); and James F. Gaines, *Social Structures in Molière's Theater* (Columbus, Ohio, 1984). Both authors are concerned with *honnêteté* not only as a social code but as a manifestation of political ideology, a tool of hegemonic control. See also Albanese, "Molière devant la socio-critique," *Visages de Molière, Ouvres et critiques* 6 (1981): 57–67. Stanton's book relates social practice to power structures in general, with an interesting application of Veblen's political theory.

25.   *Shakespearean Studies* (New York, 1927), p. 39.

CHAPTER ONE

1.   The major studies of the Restoration playhouse are Montague Summers, *The Restoration Theatre* (London, 1934), and its companion volume, *The Playhouse of Pepys* (London, 1935). Peter Holland updates Summers in his 1979 volume. For French drama an overview is furnished by John Lough in *Seventeenth-century French Drama: The Background* (Oxford, 1979).

2.   The above account is drawn largely from Summers, *Playhouse*, pp. 1–145, a thoroughly documented presentation of the life and career of both Davenant and Killigrew.

3.   Summers, *Theatre*, p. 97. The curtain is discussed exhaustively in the same volume (pp. 94–152). For the use of the stage curtain in seventeenth-century France, see Gustave Védier, *Origine et évolution de la dramaturgie classique* (Paris, 1955).

4.   The d'Orbay documents are in the archives of the Comédie-Française. Plate II dates from the 1680s, and plates III and IV are eighteenth-century illustrations derived from the "théâtre" article in the *Encyclopédie*. A comparison between plates II and III will show that very little, beyond the enlarging of the apron, was changed in the Comédie-Française playhouse between the 1680s and the 1750s. The balconies over the apron were modified to suit the new arrangement.

5.   Summers, *Theatre*, p. 57.

6.   This figure is a generalization from the 1672–73 Hubert *registre*, the only one from Molière's time that breaks down ticket sales according to the various parts of the audience space. It was published by Sylvie Chevalley in *RHT* 25 (1973): ii–195. In addition to an interpretive essay, Chevalley provides an extremely useful statistical breakdown of relevant data.

7. Roger W. Herzel, "The Decor of Molière's Stage: The Testimony of Brissart and Chauveau," *PMLA* 93 (1978): 925–54.

8. See the contract reproduced in M. Jurgens and E. Maxfield-Miller, *Cent ans de recherches sur Molière* (Paris, 1963), pp. 399–401.

9. For details on the Restoration "discovery," see Summers, *Theatre*, p. 97.

10. François d'Aubignac, *La Pratique du théâtre*, ed. Pierre Martino (Paris, 1927), pp. 43–45. First published 1657.

11. For the uninhibited conduct of the Restoration audience, see Summers, *Theatre*, pp. 67–76; John Lough, in *Paris Theatre Audiences in the Seventeenth and Eighteenth Centuries* (London, 1975), cites comparable evidence (pp. 73–117 passim).

12. The statistical data are based on Chevalley's analysis.

13. One *loge* was bought in its entirety, and fourteen separate *loge* tickets were sold. Because a *loge* could hold eight spectators and might well have been fully occupied, we can assume 22 spectators for this category.

14. A few statistical curiosities are worth appending. The spread between the highest and lowest ticket prices is greater in Paris. To sit on the stage, one would have had to pay about seven times the price of the *parterre*. In London a box cost only four times the price of a seat in the third gallery. In Paris a far greater percentage of the audience bought the lowest-priced tickets (nearly 50%), whereas only 33 of the 249 spectators for *All for Love* (13%) sat in the third gallery.

15. H. C. Lancaster, *A History of French Dramatic Literature in the Seventeenth Century* (Baltimore, 1929–42), part 5, p. 5.

CHAPTER TWO

1. Anne Ubersfeld, *Lire le théâtre* (Paris, 1978), p. 203.

2. By contrast, Corneille's early comedies map out the topography of Paris in much more detail. See my "Corneille and the Comedy of Manners."

3. See Henry Philips, *The Theatre and Its Critics in Seventeenth-Century France* (Oxford, 1980); Jonas Barish, *The Antitheatrical Prejudice* (Berkeley, Calif., 1981).

4. "De la société," in *Réflexions diverses, Maximes*, ed. J. Truchet (Paris, 1967), pp. 185–86.

5. "De la conversation," in *Réflexions diverses*, p. 191.

6. "La Lettre sur le Misanthrope," in *Les Oeuvres de Monsieur de Molière* (Paris, 1682), tome 3, pp. 99–115.

7. "Art poétique," in *Oeuvres complètes*, ed. F. Escal (Paris, 1966), p. 177.

8. Summers, *Playhouse*, pp. 284–85.

9. "General Introduction," *John Dryden: Four Comedies*, ed. L. A. Beaurline and F. Bowers (Chicago, 1967), p. 14.

10. J. H. Smith, *The Gay Couple in Restoration Comedy* (Cambridge, Mass., 1948).

CHAPTER THREE

1. Peter Brooks, *The Novel of Worldliness* (Princeton, N.J., 1969), p. 7. Brooks, it must be said, excludes Molière from the "worldly" category because, if I understand the thrust of his argument, of the comic *charge* that the playwright's dramatic and satiric bent infuses into his theater (p. 62). The contention seems to imply that a comic portrayal of worldliness is impossible, that the positive implications of satire cannot be taken into account. Jacques Morel's telling metaphor is closer to the mark: "La caricature présente comme le moule en creux de l'honnête homme" ("Molière ou la dramaturgie de l'honnêteté," *Information Littéraire* 15, 5 [1963]: 184). Brooks's very definition of a "literature of worldliness" cannot but apply, it seems to me, to the comedy of manners: "directed to man's self-conscious social existence—to know, assess, celebrate, master and give meaning to man's words and gestures as they are formed by his consciousness of society" (p. 4).

2. "Préface," in *Oeuvres complètes*, p. 2.

3. "Des biens de fortune," no. 15, in *Oeuvres complètes*, ed. J. Benda (Paris, 1957), pp. 179–80.

4. A considerable literature, and latitude of opinion, has grown up around the question of Molière's *raisonneur*, and the character type is still a matter for debate. See my "Yet Another Last Word on Molière's *Raisonneur*," *Theatre Survey* 22 (1981): 17–33.

5. In this respect Corneille's comedies are closer to Restoration norms.

6. Reproduced in Jurgens and Maxfield-Miller, *Cent ans*, pp. 566–71.

7. A. Adam, *Histoire de la littérature française au 17e siècle*, vol. 3 (Paris, 1952): 369–70.

8. Ibid., p. 383.

CHAPTER FOUR

1. F. Baumal, *Molière auteur précieux* (Paris, 1923).

2. La Bruyère, *Caractères*, "De la Mode," no. 14.

3. In fact, La Grange, though a gifted actor, was probably so typed for "straight" roles (he had been Horace in *L'Ecole des femmes* and would later play, to name a few examples, Valère in *Tartuffe*, Philinte in *Le Misanthrope*, Léandre in *Les Fourberies de Scapin*, and Clitandre in *Les Femmes savantes*) that he could well have used a little coaching in exaggeration from his master.

4. Although no indication of Oronte's social rank is given in the text of the play, he is specifically labeled an "homme de qualité" by the author of *La Lettre sur le Misanthrope* (p. 104). Molière had in mind, then, a trio of titled, affected courtiers.

CHAPTER FIVE

1.   See Susan Picinich, "Molière's Costumes as Sganarelle," *Theatre Survey* 22 (1981): 35–50.

2.   Brody's words are convincing: "Molière intended [Célimène's] unmasking, not as a defeat, but, rather, as a *déconvenue*, a momentary reversal, a pause in her progress toward elegant felicity" (*Dom Juan* and *Le Misanthrope*, p. 575).

3.   For a fuller discussion of Molière's denouements and their archetypal significance, see my *Molière*, pp. 23–24 and passim.

4.   On two occasions Molière alludes specifically to his own theater (apart, of course, from *La Critique de l'Ecole des femmes* and *L'Impromptu de Versailles*): in *Le Misanthrope* Philinte compares himself and Alceste to "ces deux frères que peint *l'Ecole des maris*" (v. 100), much to Alceste's disgust: "Mon Dieu! laissons-là vos comparaisons fades" (v. 101). Similarly, Béralde offers to take Argan to a Molière play, a suggestion that sets off the famous diatribe against that "malavisé" who dares mock medicine (*Le Malade imaginaire*, 3. 4). These mentions had special comic force for Molière's audience because the scorn for Molière came in each case from the character (Alceste, Argan) the author himself was playing.

5.   The *mouchoir* was used to cover the neck and shoulders revealed by the customary *décolleté* of women's dress at the time—whence its association, for Laurent, with the flesh.

6.   Consultations involving true professionals are caricatured in *L'Amour médecin* (2. 5); *Monsieur de Pourceaugnac* (1. 6–8); and *Le Malade imaginaire* (2. 6). Similar scenes with fake doctors take place in *L'Amour médecin* (3. 5); *Le Médecin malgré lui* (2. 4); and *Le Malade imaginaire* (3. 8–10).

CONCLUSION

1.   La Grange's annual income for 1660–73 was approximately 3,690 livres. For the 1672–73 season, he received 4,585 livres 13 sous. The extraordinary success of *Psyché* accounts largely for the good year (marred, of course, by Molière's death near the end of the season). The data on spectator categories are drawn from the tables provided in "Le Registre d'Hubert" by the editor, S. Chevalley.

2.   Quoted by P. Brooks, *The Novel of Worldliness*, p. 55. Brooks also cites the *Dictionnaire de l'Académie*: "Honnête homme ne veut dire autre chose que galant homme, homme de bonne conversation, de bonne compagnie" (ibid).

3.   Quoted by Brooks (ibid.). A modern scholar restates this primacy of social criteria: The *honnête homme* "manifeste, . . . avec ce minimum de vertu indispensable aux relations sociales, les qualités de politesse, d'esprit, de conver-

sation, de grâce" (M. Magendie, as quoted in L. Koritz, *Scarron satirique* [Paris, 1976], p. 163).

4. Although Molière often resorted to the implausible turnabout, he is faithful in *Le Misanthrope* to the realistic premises of the play: a "conversion" in Alceste such as that experienced by Manly would be unthinkable, and a marriage between Alceste and Eliante highly improbable.

5. *Les Caractères*, "Des biens de fortune," no. 27 ("Chrysippe, . . . le premier noble de sa race.")

6. For a fuller discussion, see my *Molière*, chap. 1: "Comedy: The Archetypal View."

7. *The Gondoliers*, act 2.

SELECTED BIBLIOGRAPHY

FRANCE

Molière

Primary Sources

Molière's text is standardized and available in many reliable editions; consequently I have not referred to any special one. For verse plays quotations are indicated by line number, and quotations from prose works are cited by act and scene (or scene alone for one-act plays).

Secondary Sources (Excluding Stage History)

Adam, A. *Histoire de la littérature française au 17e siècle*, vol. 3. Paris, 1952.

Albanese, Ralph, Jr. *Le Dynamisme de la peur chez Molière: une analyse socioculturelle de Dom Juan, Tartuffe, et l'Ecole des femmes.* University, Miss., 1976.

————. "Molière devant la sociocritique," in *Visages de Molière, Oeuvres et critiques* 6 (1981): 57–67.

Baumal, F. *Molière auteur précieux.* Paris, n.d. [1925].

Bénichou, Paul. *Morales du grand siècle.* Paris, 1948.

Bray, René. *Molière homme de théâtre.* Paris, 1954.

Gaines, James F. *Social Structures in Molière's Theater.* Columbus, Ohio, 1984.

Gross, Nathan. *From Gesture to Idea: Esthetics and Ethics in Molière's Comedy.* New York, 1982.

Howarth, W. D. *Molière: A Playwright and His Audience.* Cambridge, 1982.

Jurgens, M., and E. Maxfield-Miller. *Cent ans de recherches sur Molière.* Paris, 1963.

Knutson, H. C. *Molière: An Archetypal Approach.* Toronto, 1976.

————. "Yet Another Last Word on Molière's *Raisonneur.*" *Theatre Survey* 22 (1981): 17–33.

Lawrence, Francis L. "Tartuffe: A Question of *honnête* Behavior." *RN* 15 suppl. 1 (1974): 139-44.

Mesnard, J. "*Le Misanthrope*: mise en question de l'art de plaire." *RHLF* 72 (1972): 863-89.

Moore, Will G. *Molière: A New Criticism*. Oxford, 1949.

Morel, J. "Molière ou la dramaturgie de l'honnêteté." *Information littéraire* 15 (1963): 185-91.

Sweetser, M-O. "Situation de la recherche: domaines de la critique moliéresque." *Oeuvres et Critiques* 6 (1981): 9-28.

Literature Other than Molière

Primary Sources

Boileau. *Oeuvres complètes*. ed. F. Escal. Paris, 1966.

La Bruyère: *Oeuvres complètes*. ed. J. Benda. Paris, 1957.

La Rochefoucauld. *Maximes*. Ed. J. Truchet. Paris, 1967.

Secondary Sources

Brooks, Peter. *The Novel of Worldliness*. Princeton, N.J., 1969.

Dens, J-P. *L'Honnête Homme et la critique du goût: esthétique et société au XVIIe siècle*. Lexington, Ky., 1981.

Knutson, H. C. "Corneille and the Comedy of Manners," *PFSCL* 21 (1984): 393-407.

Stanton, Domna. *The Aristocrat as Art*. New York, 1980.

Theater

Primary Sources

Aubignac, François d'. *La Pratique du théâtre*. Ed. Pierre Martino. Paris, 1927.

Hubert. "Le Registre d'Hubert 1672-73." Ed. Sylvie Chevalley. *RHT* 25(1973): 1-195.

La Grange. *Le Registre de La Grange 1659-1685*. Ed. B. E. Young and G. P. Young. 2 vols. Paris, 1947.

Secondary Sources

Herzel, Roger W. "The Decor of Molière's Stage: The Testimony of Brissart and Chauveau." *PMLA* (1978): 925-54.

Lancaster, H. C. *A History of French Dramatic Literature in the Seventeenth Century*. 5 Parts, 8 Vols. Baltimore, 1929–42.

Lough, John. *Paris Theatre Audiences in the Seventeenth and Eighteenth Centuries*. London, 1975.

——. *Seventeenth-Century French Drama: The Background*. Oxford, 1979.

Phillips, Henry. *The Theatre and Its Critics in Seventeenth-Century France*. Oxford, 1980.

Picinich, S. "Molière's Costumes as Sganarelle." *Theatre Survey* 22 (1981): 35–50.

Ubersfeld, Anne. *Lire le théâtre*. Paris, 1978.

Védier, Gustave. *Origine et évolution de la dramaturgie classique*. Paris, 1955.

Social and Economic Background

A number of historical studies were consulted, among which the following were especially useful in providing a background for this study. Gaines offers a valuable summary of basic research by Mousnier and Mandrou in particular, and relates it insightfully to Molière's theater.

Goubert, Pierre. *Louis XIV et vingt millions de Français*. Paris, 1966.

——. *Initiation à l'histoire de la France*. Paris, 1984.

Mandrou, Robert. *La France au XVIIe et aux XVIIIe siècles*. Paris, 1967.

Méthivier, Hubert. *L'Ancien Régime en France*. Paris, 1981.

——. *La Fronde*. Paris, 1984.

Mousnier, Roland. *La Vénalité des offices sous Henri IV et Louis XIII*. Rouen, 1946.

——. *Les Institutions de la France sous la monarchie absolue*. Paris, 1974.

ENGLAND

Restoration Comedy

Primary Sources

As with Molière, I have not used any particular text of Etherege, Wycherley, Congreve, Farquhar, or Vanbrugh. A number of reliable editions are available.

Secondary Sources—General

Barish, Jonas. *The Antitheatrical Prejudice*. Berkeley, Calif., 1981.

Dobrée, Bonamy. *Restoration Comedy 1660–1720*. Oxford, 1924.

John Dryden: Four Comedies. Ed. L. A. Beaurline and F. Bowers. Chicago, 1967.

Fujimura, Thomas H. *The Restoration Comedy of Wit*. Princeton, N.J., 1952.

Hirst, David L. *The Comedy of Manners*. London, 1979.

Holland, Norman N. *The First Modern Comedies: The Significance of Etherege, Wycherley and Congreve*. Cambridge, Mass., 1959.

Knights, L. C. "Restoration Comedy: The Reality and the Myth," in *Explorations*. Pp. 131–49. London, 1946.

Lynch, Kathleen. *The Social Mode of Restoration Comedy*. Ann Arbor, Mich., 1926.

Muir, Kenneth. *The Comedy of Manners*. London, 1970.

Nicoll, Allardyce. *A History of Restoration Drama 1660–1700*. Pp. 168–267. Cambridge, 1923.

Palmer, John. *The Comedy of Manners*. London, 1913.

Smith, J. H. *The Gay Couple in Restoration Comedy*. Cambridge, Mass., 1948.

Stoll, E. E. *Shakespearean Studies*. New York, 1927.

Thorndyke, Ashley. *English Comedy*. New York, 1929.

Secondary Sources—Restoration Comedy and Molière

Gosse, Edmund: "Sir George Etherege: A Neglected Chapter of English Literature." *Cornhill Magazine* 42 (1881): 284–304.

Mandach, André de. *Molière et la comédie de moeurs en Angleterre 1660–68*. Neuchâtel, 1946.

Miles, D. H. *The Influence of Molière on Restoration Comedy*. New York, 1910. Reprinted 1971 as an Octagon Book.

Semple, Hilary. "Molière and Restoration Comedy." *English Studies in Africa* 18 (1975): 71–84.

Suckling, N.: "Molière and English Restoration Comedy," in *Restoration Theatre*. Ed. J. R. Brown and B. Harris. Stratford-upon-Avon Studies 6. London, 1965.

Van Laun, Henri. "Les Plagiaires de Molière en Angleterre." *Le Moliériste* 2 (1880–81) and 3 (1881–82).

Wilcox, John. *The Relation of Molière to Restoration Comedy*. New York, 1938.

Theater

Holland, Peter. *The Ornament of Action: Text and Performance in Restoration Comedy*. Cambridge, 1979.

The London Stage. Carbondale, Ill., 1960–.

Summers, Montague: *The Playhouse of Pepys*. London, 1935.

———. *The Restoration Theatre*. London, 1934.

Social and Economic Background

Kenyon, J. P. *Stuart England*. London, 1978.

Bryant, Arthur. *King Charles II*. London, 1955.

INDEX

In the list of Molière's plays, significant commentary (as opposed to passing mention) is indicated by boldface type.